Better Homes and Gardens.

Cooking Chinese

BETTER HOMES AND GARDENS® BOOKS

Editor: Gerald M. Knox
Art Director: Ernest Shelton
Managing Editor: David A. Kirchner

Food and Nutrition Editor: Doris Eby
Department Head—Cook Books: Sharyl Heiken
Senior Food Editors: Rosemary C. Hutchinson,
    Elizabeth Woolever
Senior Associate Food Editor: Sandra Granseth
Associate Food Editors: Jill Burmeister, Linda Foley,
    Linda Henry, Julia Malloy, Alethea Sparks, Marcia Stanley,
    Diane Yanney
Recipe Development Editor: Marion Viall
Test Kitchen Director: Sharon Stilwell
Test Kitchen Home Economists: Jean Brekke, Kay Cargill,
    Marilyn Cornelius, Maryellyn Krantz, Marge Steenson

Associate Art Directors: Linda Ford,
    Neoma Alt West, Randall Yontz
Copy and Production Editors: Marsha Jahns,
    Nancy Nowiszewski, Mary Helen Schiltz, David A. Walsh
Assistant Art Directors: Harijs Priekulis, Tom Wegner
Graphic Designers: Mike Burns, Alisann Dixon, Mike Eagleton,
    Lynda Haupert, Deb Miner, Lyne Neymeyer, Stan Sams,
    D. Greg Thompson, Darla Whipple, Paul Zimmerman

Editor in Chief: Neil Kuehnl
Group Editorial Services Director: Duane L. Gregg

General Manager: Fred Stines
Director of Publishing: Robert B. Nelson
Director of Retail Marketing: Jamie Martin
Director of Direct Marketing: Arthur Heydendael

COOKING CHINESE

Editor: Diane Yanney
Copy and Production Editor: David A. Walsh
Graphic Designer: D. Greg Thompson
Photographer: Mike Dieter
Illustrator: Tom Rosborough

Our seal assures you that every recipe in *Cooking Chinese* has been tested in the Better Homes and Gardens®Test Kitchen. This means that each recipe is practical and reliable, and meets our high standards of taste appeal.

On the cover: *Mix-and-Match Stir-Fry* (see recipe, pages 18 and 19).

Contents

West Meets East

If Chinese cuisine has always interested you, but its mysterious-sounding ingredients and exotic cooking methods have kept you from giving it a go in your own kitchen, relax. Just leaf through the pages of this book and you'll find that when it comes to Chinese cooking, preparing the food is as enjoyable as eating it.

Although written especially for American cooks in American kitchens, the recipes in this book are every bit as authentic as old-fashioned recipes because our versions feature characteristic Chinese flavors and traditional cooking methods—steaming, stir-frying, deep-frying, and simmering. In addition to the classics, there's a whole chapter devoted to recipes from Chinese-American restaurants—take-out favorites you can fix at home. And every now and then—just to add a dash of East-West blend—we included a recipe that combines Chinese ingredients with popular American foods.

Try a few recipes and you'll find we've taken the mystery out of the cooking with a show-and-tell approach that identifies unusual ingredients and simplifies unfamiliar cooking or preparation techniques. And, if you need help putting it all together, we've planned some hassle-free menus to give you practice in cooking and eating the Chinese way. How you choose to include Chinese cuisine in your culinary repertoire is up to you. But here are a few suggestions to get you started.

If you want to throw yourself wholeheartedly toward the Orient, eat the traditional Chinese way. Start the menu with rice—plenty of it. Rice is the star of a Chinese meal and the perfect complement to the variety of savory, salty, spicy, and sweet dishes served at the same time. Add a vegetable dish, several meat or seafood specialties (or both!), and maybe even steamed buns. Don't forget the soup— a mealtime staple and thirst quencher. Put all the food on the table at once; give each person a rice bowl, a set of chopsticks, and a soup spoon. Then let all help themselves. Save the tea for after dinner. If you must have dessert, serve fruit. (In China sweets usually are reserved for banquets or afternoon snacks.)

No time or taste for the traditional ways? Take the bits and pieces from Chinese cuisine that best suit you. Maybe just cook the Chinese way—with a steamer or wok. Or try out a recipe with exotic ingredients such as lily buds, sweet bean paste, Chinese radish, or oyster sauce. Serve an entire meal with Chinese foods but do it Western-style—eat in courses and use forks. Or make a soup, steamed buns, or Chinese sweet to add an Oriental touch to an Occidental meal. So—chopsticks or forks—create your own style using the best of West and East.

Twice-Cooked Pork

1 pound boneless pork	● Place meat in a Dutch oven; add water to cover meat. Bring to boiling; reduce heat and simmer, covered, about 45 minutes. Drain and chill, covered, in the refrigerator for 6 hours or overnight. Thinly slice pork across the grain into bite-size strips. Set aside.
1 large green *or* sweet red pepper* **1 8-ounce can bamboo shoots** **6 green onions** **2 cloves garlic** **Gingerroot**	● Cut the green or red pepper* into strips; set aside. Drain bamboo shoots well and halve lengthwise; set aside. Bias-slice onions into 1-inch-long pieces; set aside. Mince garlic; set aside. Grate 1 teaspoon gingerroot; set aside.
2 tablespoons soy sauce **2 tablespoons water** **2 tablespoons dry sherry** **1 teaspoon sugar** **Several dashes bottled hot pepper sauce**	● In a small bowl stir together the soy sauce, the water, the dry sherry, the sugar, and the hot pepper sauce; set aside soy sauce mixture.
2 tablespoons cooking oil	● Preheat wok (see tips, right) or skillet over high heat; add cooking oil. Stir-fry garlic and gingerroot in hot oil for 30 seconds. Add pepper, bamboo shoots, and onion pieces. Stir-fry for 1 minute. Remove vegetables. Add more oil if necessary. Add half of the pork to the wok or skillet. Stir-fry for 2 minutes. Remove pork. Stir-fry remaining pork for 2 minutes. Return all pork to wok or skillet. Add the vegetables. Stir the soy sauce mixture; stir into wok. Cover and cook 1 minute or just till heated through. Makes 4 to 6 servings. ***Note:** If desired, use ½ green pepper and ½ sweet red pepper.

Once you start stir-frying, it's best not to stop. So prepare all the ingredients ahead, and put them in separate bowls within easy reach of the wok.

A few stir-frying tips:
● **Add the cooking oil in a ring around the upper part of the preheated wok so it coats the sides as it runs to the wok's center.**
● **Use a spatula or long-handled spoon to stir-fry. Gently lift and turn the food with a folding motion. Keep the food moving at all times, or it will burn quickly.**
● **Push cooked food up the sides of wok before adding the soy sauce mixture. Stir the soy sauce mixture and add it to the center of the wok. Cook and stir till the mixture is bubbly. Stir all the ingredients together and heat through.**

There's more than one way to mince garlic. If you own a garlic press, you'll find it very handy. If you don't own one, a cleaver makes a good substitute (see page 50).

Oyster Sauce

Drain ½ pint *shucked oysters,* reserving the liquid. Add enough *water* to the reserved liquid to measure ½ cup. Heat oysters, the ½ cup liquid, 2 tablespoons *soy sauce,* and a few drops *Kitchen Bouquet,* if desired. Cook and stir for 3 to 5 minutes or till oysters curl. Cool. Pour the mixture into a blender container or food processor bowl. Cover; blend till smooth. Remove. Store, covered, in the refrigerator (it keeps several weeks). Note: You also can freeze the sauce. Makes 1¼ cups.

Pork in Oyster Sauce

1 pound boneless pork	● Slightly freeze pork; thinly slice across the grain into bite-size strips. Set aside.
1 cup fresh bean sprouts *or* one 16-ounce can bean sprouts **1 medium zucchini** **½ of an 8-ounce can water chestnuts** **1 small onion**	● If using canned bean sprouts; drain well. Set aside bean sprouts. Cut zucchini in half lengthwise. Slice ¼ inch thick. Set aside. Drain and thinly slice water chestnuts; set aside. Finely chop onion; set aside.
2 tablespoons water **1 tablespoon cornstarch** **3 tablespoons oyster sauce** **2 tablespoons dry sherry**	● Stir water into cornstarch. Stir in oyster sauce and dry sherry; set aside.
2 tablespoons cooking oil	● Preheat a wok (see stir-fry tips, page 7) or large skillet over high heat; add cooking oil. Stir-fry water chestnuts and bean sprouts in hot oil for 1 minute. Remove from wok. Add zucchini and onion; stir-fry for 1 minute. Remove from wok. Add more oil if necessary. Add half of the pork to the wok or skillet; stir-fry 2 to 3 minutes or till browned. Remove pork. Stir-fry remaining pork 2 to 3 minutes. Return all pork to wok or skillet. Stir oyster sauce mixture; stir into wok. Cook and stir till thickened and bubbly. Stir in vegetables. Cover and cook 1 minute. Makes 4 to 6 servings.

Even if you've never heard of oyster sauce, you won't have to search hard to find it. Most grocery stores stock it. Oyster sauce is lighter in color and thicker than soy sauce, but just as salty. You'll like the subtle flavor it adds to this pork stir-fry. If you want, make your own Oyster Sauce (see recipe, above).

Hoisin-Glazed Lamb and Asparagus

1 pound boneless lamb	● Partially freeze lamb; thinly slice into bite-size pieces. Set aside.
6 dried mushrooms	● Soak mushrooms for 30 minutes in enough warm water to cover; squeeze to drain well. Thinly slice mushrooms, discarding stems. Set aside.
2 cups fresh asparagus *or* one 10-ounce package frozen cut asparagus **3 green onions** **¼ cup sliced almonds**	● Cut fresh asparagus into 1-inch lengths; set aside. If using frozen asparagus, thaw and set aside. Thinly slice green onions; set aside. Set aside almonds.
2 tablespoons dry sherry **1 teaspoon cornstarch** **2 tablespoons hoisin sauce**	● Stir dry sherry into cornstarch. Stir in hoisin sauce; set aside.
2 tablespoons cooking oil	● Preheat wok (see stir-fry tips, page 7) or large skillet over high heat; add cooking oil. Stir-fry onion in hot oil for 1½ minutes. Add asparagus and dried mushrooms; stir-fry for 2 minutes. Remove vegetables. Add more oil if necessary. Add half of the lamb to wok or skillet; stir-fry 2 to 3 minutes. Remove lamb. Stir-fry remaining lamb 2 to 3 minutes. Return all lamb to wok or skillet.
	● Stir sherry mixture; stir into wok or skillet. Cook and stir till mixture is thickened and bubbly. Stir in vegetables and almonds. Cover and cook 1 minute. Makes 4 to 6 servings.

Some cooks call hoisin sauce the Chinese catsup. Although hoisin sauce has no real substitute, in a pinch—and for small amounts—you can use 1 part molasses to 1 part catsup (American, that is).

To bias-slice the meat, first partially freeze it (about 45 to 60 minutes for a 1-inch-thick piece). Hold a cleaver or knife at a slight angle to the cutting surface. For bite-size pieces, slice across the grain of the meat, making very thin slices (about ¹⁄₁₆ inch thick) 2 to 3 inches long.

Spicy Szechwan Beef

1 **pound beef top round steak** ½ **head bok choy** 1 **medium carrot** 1 **stalk celery** 3 **green onions**	● Partially freeze beef; slice thinly across the grain into bite-size strips. Chop the bok choy; set aside. Thinly slice the carrot; set aside. Bias-slice the celery into ½-inch lengths; set aside. Thinly slice the green onions; set aside.
2 **tablespoons dry sherry** 1 **tablespoon soy sauce** 1 **tablespoon hot bean sauce** 1 **teaspoon Hot and Peppery Oil (see recipe, page 29)** *or* **chili oil** ¾ **teaspoon Szechwan peppercorns**	● In a small bowl stir together the dry sherry, soy sauce, hot bean sauce, and Hot and Peppery Oil or chili oil. Crush the Szechwan peppercorns and add to the soy sauce mixture. Set aside.
2 **tablespoons cooking oil**	● Preheat a wok (see stir-fry tips, page 7) or large skillet over high heat; add cooking oil. Stir-fry onions for 1½ minutes. Add bok choy and celery; stir-fry 1 minute more. Add carrot; stir-fry 2 minutes more. Remove vegetables. Add more oil, if necessary. Add half of the beef to wok. Stir-fry 2 to 3 minutes. Remove beef. Stir-fry remaining beef 2 to 3 minutes. Return all meat to wok. Stir soy sauce mixture; stir into wok. Cook and stir for 1 minute or till heated through. Stir in vegetables; cover and cook 1 minute. Makes 4 to 6 servings.

Bok choy (or "Chinese cabbage") adds a sweet, mild Oriental touch to stir-frys. Its dark green leaves provide a pleasing color contrast to other ingredients.

Curried Beef and Tomato

1 **pound beef top round steak**	● Partially freeze meat; thinly slice across the grain into bite-size strips.
1 **medium cucumber** 1 **medium tomato** 1 **medium onion** 1 **clove garlic** **Gingerroot** ¾ **cup cashews** 1 **tablespoon curry powder**	● Peel cucumber; halve, seed, and thinly slice. Set aside. Peel, seed, and chop tomato; set aside. Thinly slice onion and separate into rings; set aside. Mince garlic; set aside. Grate about 1 teaspoon gingerroot; set aside. Set aside cashews and curry powder.
⅓ **cup water** 2 **teaspoons cornstarch** 1 **teaspoon instant beef bouillon granules** 1 **teaspoon sugar**	● In a small bowl stir together water, cornstarch, beef bouillon granules, and sugar. Set aside.

2 **tablespoons cooking oil**	● Preheat a wok (see stir-fry tips, page 7) or large skillet over high heat; add cooking oil. Stir-fry garlic and gingerroot in hot oil for 30 seconds. Add onion; stir-fry for 1 minute. Add cucumber and cashews. Stir-fry for 1 to 2 minutes or till nuts are just golden. Remove onion, cucumber, and nuts. Add the curry powder; stir-fry for 15 seconds or till curry is blended with oil.
	  Add more cooking oil, if necessary. Add half of the beef to wok or skillet. Stir-fry for 2 to 3 minutes or till browned. Remove beef. Stir-fry remaining beef 2 to 3 minutes. Return all beef to wok or skillet.
	  Stir the beef bouillon mixture and stir into wok. Cook and stir till thickened and bubbly. Stir in onion, cucumber, and nuts. Cover and cook 1 minute. Add tomato. Heat through. Serves 4 to 6.

Curry powder and Chinese cuisine have been around for centuries, but they didn't team up till the early 1900s when this pungent seasoning was introduced to China from India. We think you'll like the unexpected flavor and the golden glow the curry powder gives this dish.

Spicy Velveted Shrimp

12 ounces fresh *or* frozen shrimp in shells	● Thaw shrimp, if frozen. Shell and devein shrimp. Halve shrimp lengthwise.
1 egg white **1 tablespoon cornstarch** **1 teaspoon dry sherry** **½ teaspoon pepper**	● In bowl combine egg white, cornstarch, dry sherry, and pepper. By hand, work the seasonings into the shrimp; set aside.
8 ounces fresh spinach **½ of an 8-ounce can water chestnuts** **3 green onions**	● Wash, drain, and tear the spinach into bite-size pieces; set aside. Drain and thinly slice the water chestnuts; set aside. Bias-slice the onions into 1-inch pieces; set aside.
½ cup cold water **1 teaspoon cornstarch** **1 tablespoon bean sauce** **1 teaspoon sugar** **⅛ teaspoon ground red pepper**	● Stir the cold water into the cornstarch. Stir in the bean sauce, the sugar, and the ground red pepper; set aside.

2 tablespoons cooking oil	● Preheat wok (see stir-fry tips, page 7) or skillet over high heat; add *1 tablespoon* of the cooking oil. Stir-fry onion in hot oil for 1 minute. Remove onion.
	    Add the remaining 1 tablespoon cooking oil. Add shrimp to wok or skillet; stir-fry 2 to 3 minutes.
	    Stir bean sauce mixture; stir into wok or skillet. Cook and stir till thickened and bubbly. Stir in spinach, water chestnuts, and onions. Cover and cook 1 minute. Makes 4 to 6 servings.
	Note: The egg white-cornstarch mixture you work into the shrimp is what makes them "velveted." This Chinese coating technique keeps food tender with a smooth, soft texture.

Using a sharp knife, make a shallow slit along the backs of the shrimp. Look for the vein, which will appear as a dark line, running down the center of the shrimp's back. If a vein is present, use the tip of the knife to scrape out the vein; discard it.

Scallop and Vegetable Stir-Fry

2 **tablespoons dried lily buds** 1 **pound fresh *or* frozen scallops**	● Soak lily buds for 30 minutes in enough warm water to cover; squeeze to drain well. Cut lily buds into 1-inch lengths; set aside. Thaw scallops if frozen. Halve scallops; set aside.
2 **cups fresh green beans** 1 **medium onion** **Fresh coriander *or* parsley** **Gingerroot**	● Bias-slice green beans into 1-inch lengths. In covered saucepan cook green beans in boiling salted water for 5 minutes; drain well and set aside. Chop onion; set aside. Snip 2 tablespoons coriander; set aside. Grate ½ teaspoon gingerroot; set aside.
½ **cup unsweetened pineapple juice** 2 **teaspoons cornstarch** 1 **tablespoon soy sauce**	● Stir pineapple juice into cornstarch; stir in soy sauce. Set aside.
2 **tablespoons cooking oil**	● Preheat a wok (see stir-fry tips, page 7) or skillet over high heat; add oil. Stir-fry the onion and gingerroot in hot oil for 1 minute. Add the green beans and lily buds; stir-fry 2 minutes. Remove the vegetables. Add more oil, if necessary. Add half of the scallops to wok or skillet. Stir-fry 2 to 3 minutes. Remove the scallops. Stir-fry the remaining scallops 2 to 3 minutes; return all scallops to the wok or skillet. Stir the pineapple juice mixture; stir into the wok or skillet. Cook and stir till thickened and bubbly. Stir in cooked vegetables, and coriander or parsley. Cook and stir 1 minute more or till heated through. Makes 4 to 6 servings.

Lily buds (top), dried mushrooms (center), and tree ears (bottom) come to life after soaking. Lily buds are sold as tiger-lily buds or golden needles; **dried mushrooms are also known as fragrant mushrooms; and tree ears are also called wood ears, cloud ears, or jelly mushrooms.**

Chicken on Lettuce

1 **whole large chicken breast**	● Skin, halve lengthwise, and bone chicken; finely chop and set aside.

mushrooms

¼ **cup slivered almonds** ~~almonds~~ *peanuts*	● Finely chop almonds; set aside. Thinly slice green onions; set aside. Set aside bean sprouts.
2 **green onions**	
¼ **cup fresh bean sprouts**	

Cabbage - angel hair

2 **tablespoons dry white wine**	● Stir 2 tablespoons white wine into cornstarch. Stir in soy sauce and ginger; set aside.
2 **teaspoons cornstarch**	
1 **tablespoon soy sauce**	
⅛ **teaspoon** ~~ground~~ **ginger** *fresh*	

2 **tablespoons cooking oil**	● Preheat a wok (see stir-fry tips, page 7) or large skillet over high heat; add oil. Stir-fry onions in hot oil 1 minute. Add almonds and bean sprouts; stir-fry 1½ minutes. Remove vegetables and nuts. Add chicken to wok or skillet. Stir-fry for 2 minutes. Add onions, almonds, and bean sprouts. Stir wine mixture; stir into chicken mixture. Cook and stir till bubbly. Cook 2 minutes more. For dipping sauce, combine hoisin sauce, 2 tablespoons white wine, and water.
¼ **cup hoisin sauce**	
2 **tablespoons dry white wine**	
1 **tablespoon water**	

12 **small romaine leaves** *or* **leaf lettuce leaves**	● If using romaine leaves, remove stem end of heavy center vein from leaves. To assemble, spoon one rounded tablespoon mixture in center of each leaf. Fold up leaf from bottom to center of leaf. Fold in two sides of leaf so they overlap about 1 inch over filling. Pass dipping sauce. Dip lettuce bundles in sauce for each bite. Serves 4.

water chestnuts
crushed pepper (red)
sesame oil - drizzle
Bibb lettuce

So you think you're an expert with chopsticks. Try eating this the Chinese way. Use chopsticks to place the filling on the lettuce and fold the bundle. Then use your chopsticks to pick up the bundle and dip it in the sauce. If chopsticks aren't for you, follow these more conventional directions.

Place chicken mixture in center of lettuce leaf. Fold up leaf from bottom to center.

Fold in two sides of leaf so they overlap about 1 inch over the filling.

heat. Add onion; cook 4 minutes or until tender. Add nectarine, cranberries, and vinegar; cook 3 minutes or until nectarine is tender. Remove from heat; stir in ¼ teaspoon salt, cinnamon, cloves, and remaining 2 teaspoons butter.

2. To prepare pork, cut pork crosswise into 8 (1-inch-thick) slices. Place each slice between 2 sheets of heavy-duty plastic wrap; pound to ½-inch thickness using a meat mallet or small heavy skillet. Sprinkle pork evenly with ½ teaspoon salt and pepper. Heat a large nonstick skillet over medium-high heat. Coat pan with cooking spray. Add pork; cook 3 minutes on each side or until desired degree of doneness. Serve pork with chutney. Yield: 4 servings (serving size: 2 pork slices and about ⅓ cup chutney).

CALORIES 233 (29% from fat); FAT 7.6g (sat 3.4g, mono 2.8g, poly 0.7g); PROTEIN 18.4g; CARB 23.1g; FIBER 1.6g; CHOL 64mg; IRON 1.4mg; SODIUM 507mg; CALC 12mg

Chicken Lettuce Wraps with Sweet and Spicy Sauce

You can serve these casual wraps buffet style. Arrange the lettuce leaves on a large platter, spoon the chicken salad in a bowl, and place the sauce in a small bowl on the side. Let people assemble their own wraps since this is one less step for the cook.

- 3 tablespoons unsalted, dry-roasted peanuts
- 3 tablespoons hoisin sauce
- 2 tablespoons cider vinegar
- 2 teaspoons low-sodium soy sauce
- 1 teaspoon bottled ground fresh ginger (such as Spice World)
- 1 teaspoon dark sesame oil
- ½ teaspoon crushed red pepper
- ½ teaspoon bottled minced garlic
- 2 cups packaged cabbage-and-carrot coleslaw
- 1 cup canned sliced water chestnuts, drained
- 8 ounces grilled chicken breast strips (such as Louis Rich)
- 12 Bibb lettuce leaves

1. Place peanuts in a small nonstick skillet over medium-high heat; cook 3 minutes or until lightly browned, shaking pan frequently. Remove pan from heat; set aside.

2. Combine hoisin, vinegar, soy sauce, ginger, oil, pepper, and garlic in a small bowl, stirring well with a whisk.

3. Combine peanuts, coleslaw, water chestnuts, and chicken in a medium bowl; toss well.

4. Spoon about ⅓ cup chicken salad in the center of each lettuce leaf; top each with 2 teaspoons sauce. Roll up; secure with a wooden pick. Yield: 4 servings (serving size: 3 wraps).

CALORIES 197 (34% from fat); FAT 7.4g (sat 1.4g, mono 2.9g, poly 2.1g); PROTEIN 16.5g; CARB 18.2g; FIBER 3.4g; CHOL 37mg; IRON 1.9mg; SODIUM 825mg; CALC 40mg

Summer Black Bean and Pasta Salad

Drain the pasta, and rinse it immediately with cold water to cool it quickly. If you can't find ditalini pasta, substitute tubetti or small elbow macaroni.

- ¾ cup uncooked ditalini (very short tube-shaped macaroni, 3 ounces)
- 1½ cups halved grape tomatoes
- ¾ cup diced peeled avocado
- ½ cup chopped seeded poblano chile (about 1)
- ½ cup chopped cucumber
- ⅓ cup chopped red onion
- 2 tablespoons chopped fresh cilantro
- 1 (15-ounce) can black beans, drained and rinsed
- 2 teaspoons grated lime rind
- 2 tablespoons fresh lime juice
- 1 tablespoon cider vinegar
- 2 teaspoons extravirgin olive oil
- ¾ teaspoon bottled minced garlic
- ¾ teaspoon salt
- ⅛ teaspoon ground red pepper
- 1 medium lime, cut in 4 wedges

1. Cook pasta according to package directions, omitting salt and fat. Drain and cool completely.

2. Combine the tomatoes, avocado, poblano, cucumber, onion, cilantro, and beans in a medium bowl, stirring well. Combine rind, juice, vinegar, oil, garlic, salt, and pepper in a small bowl, stirring well with a whisk. Add pasta and lime mixture to bean mixture; toss to combine. Serve with lime wedges. Yield: 4 servings (serving size: 1½ cups pasta and 1 lime wedge).

CALORIES 214 (30% from fat); FAT 7.1g (sat 1.1g, mono 4.4g, poly 0.9g); PROTEIN 7.3g; CARB 35.5g; FIBER 7.2g; CHOL 0mg; IRON 2.4mg; SODIUM 656mg; CALC 47mg

Recipes by Melanie Barnard, Allison Fishman, Nancy Hughes, and Karen Levin.

3. To prepare cake, coat bottoms of 3 (8-inch) round cake pans with cooking spray (do not coat sides of pans); line bottoms with wax paper. Coat wax paper with cooking spray; dust with 1 tablespoon flour.

4. Lightly spoon 2 cups cake flour into dry measuring cups, and level with a knife. Combine 2 cups cake flour, 1 cup sugar, baking powder, and ½ teaspoon salt in a large bowl, stirring with a whisk until well combined.

5. Combine oil, ⅓ cup juice, 3 tablespoons water, 1 teaspoon rind, lemon extract, and egg yolks in a medium bowl, stirring with a whisk. Add oil mixture to flour mixture; beat with a mixer at medium speed until smooth.

6. Place egg whites in a large bowl; beat with a mixer at high speed until foamy. Add cream of tartar; beat until soft peaks form. Gradually add remaining ¼ cup sugar, 1 tablespoon at a time, beating until stiff peaks form. Gently stir one-fourth of egg white mixture into flour mixture; gently fold in remaining egg white mixture.

7. Divide cake batter equally among prepared pans, spreading evenly. Break air pockets by cutting through batter with a knife. Bake at 325° for 20 minutes or until cake springs back when lightly touched. Cool in pans for 10 minutes on a wire rack; remove from pans. Remove wax paper from cake layers. Cool completely on wire rack.

8. To prepare frosting, combine 3 tablespoons sugar and 2 tablespoons lime juice in a small glass bowl. Microwave at HIGH for 30 seconds or until sugar dissolves. Cool completely. Fold into whipped topping.

9. To assemble cake, place 1 cake layer on a plate; spread half of filling over cake layer. Top with second layer, remaining half of filling, and third layer. Spread frosting over top and sides of cake. Garnish with mint, blueberries, and lime wedges, if desired. Store cake loosely covered in refrigerator for up to 3 days. Slice cake into wedges. Yield: 16 servings (serving size: 1 slice).

CALORIES 290 (29% from fat); FAT 9.3g (sat 2.1g, mono 4.6g, poly 2.1g); PROTEIN 5.3g; CARB 44.9g; FIBER 0.3g; CHOL 47mg; IRON 1.1mg; SODIUM 218mg; CALC 122mg

Jan Moon is a Cooking Light Test Kitchens professional.

LIFE
TAKES
PAPERWORK

The Beauville Times

LIFE
TAKES
VISA

VISA CHECK CARD
4000 1234 5678 9010
2005 12/08
L. SCOTT
DEBIT
VISA

With the Visa Check Card, paying your bills is like a day at the beach. Pay bills like your phone, cable and utilities, quickly and conveniently, online or by phone. And take some time to kick up your heels. Go to visa.com/billpay to get what it takes.

Five Spice Chicken and Vegetables

2 whole large chicken breasts 3 tablespoons soy sauce ¼ teaspoon five spice powder *or* Homemade Five Spice Powder (see recipe, right)	● Skin, halve lengthwise, and bone chicken breasts; cut into 1-inch pieces. Combine chicken, soy sauce, and five spice powder; let stand 15 minutes at room temperature.
1 medium zucchini 1 large carrot 1 medium onion	● Quarter zucchini lengthwise and cut into ½-inch pieces. Bias-slice carrot into 1-inch-thick slices. Thinly slice onion; separate into rings. Set vegetables aside.
¼ cup chicken broth 2 teaspoons cornstarch	● Blend chicken broth into cornstarch. Set aside.
2 tablespoons cooking oil	● Preheat a wok (see stir-fry tips, page 7) or large skillet over high heat; add oil. Stir-fry carrots in hot oil for 1 minute. Add onion and zucchini; stir-fry 2 minutes or till crisp-tender. Remove vegetables. Add more oil if necessary. Add half the chicken mixture to wok; stir-fry 2 minutes. Remove. Stir-fry remaining chicken mixture for 2 minutes. Return all chicken mixture to wok. Stir broth mixture and stir into chicken. Cook and stir till bubbly. Stir in vegetables. Cover; cook 1 minute. Serves 4 to 6.

You'll find five spice powder in your grocery store's Oriental foods section or at an Oriental market. If you like, make your own *Homemade Five Spice Powder*. Here's how:
  Combine 1 teaspoon ground *cinnamon;* 1 teaspoon crushed *aniseed or* 1 *star anise,* ground; ¼ teaspoon crushed *fennel seed;* ¼ teaspoon freshly ground *pepper* or ¼ teaspoon *Szechwan pepper;* and ⅛ teaspoon ground *cloves.* Store in covered container.

Hold chicken breast half with bone side down. Starting from the breastbone, use a sharp knife to cut meat away from the bone.

Cut with a sawing motion, pressing the flat side of the knife blade against the rib bones. With the other hand, gently pull meat away from rib bones.

Vegetable Stir-Fry

½ medium head broccoli	● Cut broccoli into 1-inch pieces. In a saucepan cook the broccoli, covered, in boiling salted water 2 to 3 minutes. Drain; set aside.
½ head bok choy 2 cups cauliflower flowerets 1 cup fresh mushrooms 1 medium onion ½ cup radishes 4 ounces fresh bean curd (tofu) ¼ cup chicken broth 2 tablespoons soy sauce 2 tablespoons dry white wine	● Chop bok choy; set aside. Thinly slice cauliflower; set aside. Thinly slice mushrooms; set aside. Thinly slice onion and separate into rings; set aside. Thinly slice radishes; set aside. Cube bean curd; place into a small bowl. For marinade, combine chicken broth, soy sauce, and wine. Mix well and pour over bean curd. Let stand 30 minutes. Drain, reserving marinade.
2 teaspoons cornstarch ¼ teaspoon pepper	● Add the cornstarch and the pepper to the reserved marinade.
2 tablespoons cooking oil	● Preheat a wok (see stir-fry tips, page 7) or large skillet over high heat; add oil. Stir-fry onion in hot oil for 2 minutes. Remove onion. Add mushrooms and bok choy. Stir-fry 2 minutes; remove from wok. Add more oil, if necessary. Add broccoli and cauliflower. Stir-fry 2 to 3 minutes. Add mushrooms, onions, and bok choy. Stir marinade mixture; stir into wok. Cook and stir till bubbly. Add bean curd and radishes; cover and cook 1 minute more. Serves 4 to 6.

Red radish adds a bright spot of color to this stir-fry; but you might want to try the more traditional white radish or daikon (above, left), too. Bean curd (above, right)—also called tofu—is best used soon after purchase. Drain and rinse leftover tofu. Cover with water; refrigerate in covered container. Drain and change water daily.

Curried Vegetable Stir-Fry

1 medium carrot	● Bias-slice the carrot into 1-inch pieces. Cook in boiling salted water 10 to 15 minutes or till pieces are crisp-tender. Drain; set aside.
3 medium cucumbers *or* zucchini	
1 medium tomato	Halve cucumbers or zucchini lengthwise; trim ends and scoop out seeds. Cut seeded cucumbers or zucchini into ¼-inch slices; set aside. Core tomato and cut into thin wedges; set aside. Thinly slice onion; separate into rings. Set aside. Mince garlic; set aside.
1 medium onion	
1 clove garlic	

¼ cup soy sauce	● In a small bowl stir soy sauce into cornstarch. Add sugar; set aside.
2 teaspoons cornstarch	
1 teaspoon sugar	

2 tablespoons cooking oil	● Preheat a wok (see stir-fry tips, page 7) or large skillet over high heat. Add cooking oil. Stir-fry onion and garlic in hot oil for 3 minutes. Sprinkle with curry powder; stir-fry 1 minute more.
1 tablespoon curry powder	

Add cucumbers or zucchini to wok or skillet; stir-fry 5 to 7 minutes or till crisp-tender. Stir soy mixture; stir into wok. Cook until thickened and bubbly. Add carrot and tomato. Cover and cook 1 to 2 minutes more or till heated through. Makes 4 to 6 servings.

The first time we tested this recipe, we used shredded carrot so it would cook fast in the wok without pre-cooking. But it just didn't look right. So we switched to carrot chunks to make the ingredients look better together. In Chinese cooking, the appearance of a dish is just as important as its taste.

What we've put down on paper is information that is second nature for Chinese cooks—how to put almost any variety of ingredients together in a stir-fry. Pick and choose as you please, the possibilities are endless. Select one ingredient from each column— except for the Basics, all of which belong in every Mix-and-Match Stir-Fry. With this chart as a guide you can create main-dish masterpieces from what you have on hand—just as Chinese cooks do.

Meat/Fish	+ Vegetables I	+ Vegetables II
1 pound fresh *or* frozen medium shrimp in shells, thawed, peeled and deveined	**2 large carrots, thinly bias sliced**	**2 cups chopped Chinese cabbage**
1 pound boneless pork, partially frozen and thinly sliced into bite-size strips	**1 cup broccoli buds**	**1 cup fresh pea pods, halved lengthwise**
	1 cup fresh asparagus cut into 1-inch lengths	**1 cup fresh mushrooms thinly sliced**
2 whole large chicken breasts, skinned, halved lengthwise, boned, and cut into 1-inch pieces	**½ cup cauliflower flowerets, thinly sliced**	**2 medium tomatoes, cut into wedges and seeded**
1 pound beef top round steak, partially frozen and thinly sliced into bite-size pieces		

Crunchy
\+ Ingredients

1 **8-ounce can
water chest-
nuts, drained
and thinly
sliced**

1 **cup walnut
pieces**

1 **cup dry-roasted
peanuts**

2 **stalks celery,
thinly sliced**

\+ Basics

⅓ **cup cold water**

2 **teaspoons cornstarch**

2 **tablespoons soy sauce**

1 **tablespoon dry sherry**

2 **tablespoons cooking oil**

1 **clove garlic, minced**

4 **green onions, thinly sliced**

½ **cup fresh bean sprouts *or*
canned bean sprouts,
drained, *or* one-half of an
8-ounce can bamboo
shoots, drained (optional)**

Mix-and-Match Stir-Fry

● Prepare your choice of ingredients
from Meat/Fish and Vegetables I and II
categories; set aside. Stir water into
cornstarch; stir in soy sauce and sherry.
Set aside.

● In covered saucepan cook Vegetable I
in boiling salted water for 3 minutes.
Drain well; set aside. Preheat wok (see
stir-fry tips, page 7) or large skillet over
high heat; add cooking oil. Stir-fry garlic
in hot oil for 30 seconds. Add green
onions and stir-fry 1 minute.

● Add Crunchy Ingredient and bean
sprouts or bamboo shoots. Stir-fry 1 to 2
minutes. Remove from wok. Add Vegetables I and II. Stir-fry 1 minute. Remove
from wok.

● Add more oil, if necessary. Add half
of the Meat/Fish to wok or skillet; stir-fry
2 to 3 minutes or till browned. Remove
Meat/Fish. Stir-fry remaining Meat/Fish
2 to 3 minutes. Return all Meat/Fish to
wok. Add Crunchy Ingredient and bean
sprouts or bamboo shoots.

● Stir soy sauce mixture; stir into wok.
Cook and stir till thickened and bubbly.
Return Vegetables I and II to wok; cover
and cook 1 minute more.

● Serve atop deep-fried rice sticks or
with rice, if desired. Serves 4 to 6.

Deep-Fried Meatballs

1 slightly beaten egg
1 tablespoon dry sherry
¾ cup soft bread crumbs
¼ cup finely chopped celery
2 tablespoons finely
    chopped green onion
2 tablespoons snipped
    parsley
1 teaspoon grated
    gingerroot
½ teaspoon prepared
    mustard
¼ teaspoon salt
1 pound ground beef
    All-purpose flour

● In a bowl combine the beaten egg and dry sherry. Stir in the soft bread crumbs, the finely chopped celery, the finely chopped green onion, the chopped parsley, the grated gingerroot, the prepared mustard, and salt. Add ground beef. Mix all ingredients thoroughly.

Shape the mixture into balls, using about 2 tablespoons for each. Roll the balls in flour to lightly coat.

Roasted Szechwan Salt-Pepper: In a heavy skillet combine 3 tablespoons *salt* and 1 tablespoon *Szechwan peppercorns.* Cook over medium heat, stirring constantly, for 3 to 5 minutes or till peppers begin to smoke slightly and salt is lightly browned. Remove from heat; cool. With a mortar and pestle or a rolling pin, crush salt and peppercorns. Pass the salt-pepper mixture through a sieve to remove peppercorn husks. Store in a tightly covered jar. Makes about ¼ cup.

Cooking oil for deep-fat
    frying
Roasted Szechwan Salt-
    Pepper (see recipe,
    right) *or* Mustard Sauce
    (see recipe, page 24)

● Fry the balls, several at a time, in deep hot oil (365°) about 2 minutes or till golden. Remove with a strainer or slotted spoon. Drain on paper toweling. Keep warm while frying remaining balls. Serve with Roasted Szechwan Salt-Pepper or Mustard Sauce. Serves 4 to 6.

Deep-Fat Frying

To deep-fry in a wok, place the wok securely on its ring stand. Then add 1 to 1½ inches of cooking oil (3 to 4 cups). Attach a deep-fat frying thermometer to the side of the wok. Heat the oil to the required temperature. (Watch the oil temperature closely. If it's too low, the food will be greasy; too high and the food will burn before it cooks.) Use a wire strainer or slotted spoon to add food to the hot oil. Fry food in small batches, because too much food will lower the oil's temperature. Be sure oil returns to the right temperature between batches. Drain the food on a rack (see photo) or use paper toweling. Let the wok cool completely before removing the oil. If desired, strain oil through two layers of cheesecloth into jars. Cover tightly; refrigerate.

Deep-Fried Chicken Wings

12 chicken wings

● Cut off and discard tips of chicken wings. Cut wings at joints to form 24 pieces. Place on shallow baking pan. Bake in a 350° oven for 20 minutes.

To prepare chicken wings for frying, cut off their wing tips and discard. Then chop the chicken wings in two at the joints.

1 beaten egg
3 tablespoons cornstarch
3 tablespoons all-purpose flour
2 tablespoons soy sauce
2 tablespoons dry sherry
1 tablespoon honey
½ teaspoon garlic powder
½ teaspoon Roasted Szechwan Salt-Pepper (see recipe, opposite)
Cooking oil for deep-fat frying

● In a mixing bowl stir together the beaten egg, the cornstarch, the all-purpose flour, the soy sauce, the dry sherry, the honey, the garlic powder, and the Roasted Szechwan Salt-Pepper. Beat till smooth.

Dip chicken wing pieces in batter. Fry wing pieces, a few at a time, in deep hot cooking oil (365°) for 1 minute or till golden brown. Drain on paper toweling. Keep warm while cooking remaining wings. Makes 24.

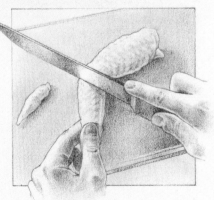

Egg Rolls

1 Place egg roll skin with one point toward you.

2 Spoon the filling diagonally across and just below center of egg roll skin. Fold bottom point of skin over filling.

3 Tuck point under filling. Fold side corners over, forming an envelope shape. Roll up egg roll toward remaining corner; moisten point and press firmly to seal. To fry, see step 4 opposite.

Vegetable Filling

⅔ cup shredded zucchini
⅔ cup shredded carrot
⅔ cup finely chopped mushrooms
½ cup finely chopped onion
½ cup finely chopped green pepper
⅓ cup ground peanuts
2 tablespoons soy sauce
¼ teaspoon sugar
¼ teaspoon pepper

● In mixing bowl, combine the shredded zucchini, the shredded carrot, the finely chopped mushrooms, the finely chopped onion, the finely chopped green pepper, the ground peanuts, the soy sauce, the sugar, and the pepper; mix well.

Few foods are worse than cold egg rolls. To serve these popular appetizers piping hot, drain them on paper toweling after frying. Then place on a baking sheet lined with paper toweling, and keep toasty and crisp in a 300° oven till you've deep-fried the whole batch.

12 egg roll skins *or* 48 wonton skins

● Fill and fry the egg rolls using directions above or the wontons using directions at right. Serve the egg rolls or wontons warm with one or two sauces (see suggestions, page 26). Makes 12 egg rolls or 48 wontons.

Wontons

By themselves, wontons may seem pretty humble; but their versatility is hard to beat. With meat or vegetable fillings, they can be deep-fried for appetizers or boiled for soup (see recipe, page 54). When deep-fried with a sweet filling, wontons become an exotic dessert (see recipe, page 75).

Position wonton skin with one point toward you.

Spoon filling just off center of skin. Fold bottom point of wonton skin over the filling. Tuck point under filling.

Roll to cover filling, leaving 1-inch unrolled at top of the skin.

Moisten right corner of skin with water. Grasp corners and bring them toward you below filling. Lap right corner over left corner. Press to seal. To fry, see directions at right.

4 Fry egg rolls or wontons, a few at a time, in deep hot oil (365°) for 2 to 3 minutes or till golden brown. Drain on paper toweling.

Chicken and Shrimp Filling

1 whole small chicken breast	● Skin, halve lengthwise, and bone chicken; finely chop.
¼ cup chopped onion **1 tablespoon cooking oil** **1½ cups chopped Chinese cabbage *or* cabbage** **1 cup fresh *or* canned bean sprouts, drained**	● In wok or skillet, stir-fry onion in hot cooking oil for 1 minute. Add chicken; stir-fry for 2 minutes. Add cabbage and bean sprouts; stir-fry about 3 minutes more. Remove from heat; cool slightly.
1 4½-ounce can shrimp, drained and chopped **1 beaten egg** **2 tablespoons dry white wine *or* water** **⅛ teaspoon five spice powder *or* Homemade Five Spice Powder (see recipe, page 15)**	● In a mixing bowl combine the drained and chopped shrimp, the chicken-vegetable mixture, the beaten egg, the dry white wine or water, and the five spice powder or the Homemade Five Spice Powder.
10 egg roll skins *or* 40 wonton skins	● Wrap, fry, and serve the egg rolls or the wontons using the directions on pages 22 and 23. Makes 10 egg rolls or 40 wontons.

Let your cleaver do the fine chopping for egg roll, wonton, and potsticker fillings. First, cut meat, poultry, or seafood into small pieces. Then gather them together on the cutting board. Hold the cleaver perpendicular to the cutting board and move it up and down in straight cutting motions from one side of the meat pieces to the other. With the flat side of the cleaver, scoop up the meat and flip it over. Repeat the chopping motion till the meat is finely chopped—almost ground. Occasionally rinse the cleaver with cold water to keep the meat from sticking.

Mustard Sauce

¼ cup water **¼ cup dry mustard** **1 teaspoon sesame oil *or* cooking oil**	● In small saucepan bring water to boiling. Combine mustard and sesame oil. Stir boiling water into mustard mixture. Makes about ⅓ cup sauce.
	Hot and Spicy Mustard: Prepare as above, except substitute ½ teaspoon *Hot and Peppery Oil* (see recipe, page 29) or *chili oil* for the 1 teaspoon sesame oil or cooking oil.

A little goes a long way—when it comes to using sesame oil. This distinctive Chinese ingredient has a stronger flavor than other cooking oils. Buy a bottle and share it with fellow cooks who enjoy Oriental foods.

Crab and Ham Filling

¼ **cup dried tree ears** ½ **cup hot water**	● In small bowl cover tree ears with hot water. Let soak for 30 minutes. Rinse and squeeze to drain thoroughly. Finely chop the tree ears; set aside.

½ **of a 10-ounce package**
   frozen chopped spinach
1 **beaten egg**
1 **cup finely chopped fully**
   cooked ham
1 **6-ounce can crab meat,**
   drained, flaked, and
   cartilage removed
	● Thaw and drain the spinach well. For the filling, in a large mixing bowl stir together the beaten egg, the finely chopped ham, the drained and flaked crab meat, the chopped tree ears, and the drained spinach.

2 **tablespoons orange juice** 2 **teaspoons cornstarch**	● Stir orange juice into cornstarch. Stir into filling mixture.
9 **egg roll skins** *or* **36** **wonton skins**	● Wrap, fry, and serve the egg rolls or the wontons using the directions on pages 22 and 23. Makes 9 egg rolls or 36 wontons.

Sneak a peek to page 54 and you'll find another good use for this yummy Crab and Ham Filling. Besides being a classy stuffing for fried egg rolls or wontons, it makes dressed-up dumplings for Wonton Soup.

Roast Pork Filling

2 tablespoons soy sauce 1 tablespoon orange juice 2 teaspoons cornstarch	● Blend soy sauce and orange juice into cornstarch; set aside.
1½ cups fresh bean sprouts *or* canned bean sprouts, drained 1 cup finely chopped **Chinese Roast Pork (see recipe, page 62)** *or* **finely chopped cooked pork** ½ cup finely chopped **walnuts** *or* **almonds** ¼ cup sliced **green onion**	● Coarsely chop the bean sprouts. In a bowl combine the finely chopped Chinese Roast Pork or cooked pork, the coarsely chopped bean sprouts, the finely chopped walnuts or almonds, and the sliced green onion. Stir the soy sauce mixture into the pork mixture.
10 egg roll skins *or* 40 wonton skins	● Wrap, fry, and serve the egg rolls or the wontons using the directions on pages 22 and 23. Makes 10 egg rolls or 40 wontons.

Egg rolls and wontons are dull without a sauce. Make up one or two to serve on the side. Choose from *Mustard Sauce* (see recipe, page 24), *Sweet and Sour Sauce* (see recipe below), *Soy-Vinegar Dipping Sauce* (see recipe, page 84), or (if your tongue can stand it) *Hot and Peppery Dipping Sauce* (see recipe, page 29).

**   Purchased sauces from your Oriental market will fill the bill, too.**

Sweet and Sour Sauce

In a small saucepan combine ½ cup packed *brown sugar* and 1 tablespoon *cornstarch*. Stir in ⅓ cup *chicken broth,* ⅓ cup *red wine vinegar,* 1 tablespoon *soy sauce,* 1 teaspoon grated *gingerroot,* and 2 cloves *garlic,* minced. Cook and stir till thickened and bubbly. Cook and stir 2 minutes more. Serve warm or cold with egg rolls or wontons. Makes about 1 cup.

Beef and Bacon Filling

4 slices bacon
1 pound ground beef
¼ cup sliced green onion
2 tablespoons finely chopped green pepper

● In skillet cook bacon till crisp. Drain off fat. Crumble bacon and set aside. In same skillet cook ground beef, onion, and green pepper till vegetables are tender and meat is browned.

Here's a real twist to the traditional egg roll filling. We added one of our favorite ingredients from the East (hoisin sauce) and one from the West (bacon) and came up with a simply superb egg roll.

⅓ cup finely chopped water chestnuts
1 tablespoon hoisin sauce
1 tablespoon soy sauce

● Stir in water chestnuts, hoisin sauce, and soy sauce; mix well. Stir in bacon.

6 egg roll skins *or* 24 wonton skins

● Wrap, fry, and serve the egg rolls or the wontons using the directions on pages 22 and 23. Makes 6 egg rolls or 24 wontons.

Lamb-Curry Filling

1 pound ground lamb
1 beaten egg
1 cup chopped bok choy
½ cup finely chopped bamboo shoots
¼ cup chopped onion
1 teaspoon curry powder
½ teaspoon salt
1 clove garlic, minced

● In a large mixing bowl combine the ground lamb, the beaten egg, the chopped bok choy, the chopped bamboo shoots, the chopped onion, the curry powder, the salt, and the minced garlic. Mix well.

When you want wontons in the worst way, but you can't find wonton skins, substitute egg roll skins. Cut ten egg roll skins into quarters and you'll have forty wonton-size skins.

10 egg rolls skins *or* 40 wonton skins

● Wrap, fry, and serve the egg rolls or the wontons using the directions on pages 22 and 23. Makes 10 egg rolls or 40 wontons.

Chinese Potstickers

3 cups all-purpose flour
½ teaspoon salt
1 cup boiling water
⅓ cup cold water
¼ cup all-purpose flour

● To prepare the dumpling dough, in a bowl stir together the 3 cups flour and the salt. Pour the boiling water slowly into flour, stirring constantly. Stir till well blended. Stir in the cold water.

When cool enough to handle, knead dough on a well-floured surface, kneading in the ¼ cup flour till dough is smooth and elastic (8 to 10 minutes). Shape dough into a ball. Place dough back into bowl; cover with a damp towel. Let stand for 15 to 20 minutes.

Spoon about 1 tablespoon filling in the center of each dough round. Fold round in half across filling, pleating one edge of dough to smoothly fit against opposite edge; pinch edges to seal. Set sealed edge of dumpling upright and press gently to slightly flatten the bottom.

Pork and Vegetable Filling *or* Beef and Vegetable Filling (see recipes, opposite)

● Turn dough out onto a lightly floured surface. Divide dough into four equal portions. Roll each portion to ⅛-inch thickness. With a cookie cutter, cut into 3-inch rounds, making about 45 rounds (reroll as needed).

Spoon about 1 tablespoon of filling in the center of one round. Fold round in half across filling and pinch edges to seal. Set sealed edge of potsticker upright and press gently to slightly flatten the bottom. Transfer to a floured baking sheet. Cover with a dry towel. Repeat with the remaining filling and rounds.

**Cooking oil
Water
Soy-Vinegar Dipping Sauce (see recipe, page 84) *or* Hot-and-Peppery Dipping Sauce (see recipe, opposite far right)**

● In a 12-inch skillet heat 2 tablespoons oil about 1 minute or till very hot. Set *half* of the potstickers upright in skillet (making sure potstickers do not touch each other); cook in hot oil about 1 minute or till bottoms are lightly browned. Reduce heat. Add ⅔ *cup* water to skillet. Cover; cook about 10 minutes. Uncover and cook 2 to 3 minutes or till all water evaporates. Cook potstickers, uncovered, for 1 minute more. Using a wide spatula gently remove potstickers from skillet. Keep potstickers warm while cooking remaining potstickers. Serve with Soy-Vinegar Dipping Sauce or Hot-and-Peppery Dipping Sauce. Makes 45.

Beef and Vegetable Filling

1 **pound ground beef** ¼ **cup thinly sliced green onion** ¼ **cup finely chopped green pepper**	● In a skillet, cook ground beef, onion, and green pepper till beef is brown and onion is tender, stirring often to break up pieces of meat. Drain off fat.	**If you have a strong constitution and love hot foods, serve this pungent sauce with potstickers.** *Hot-and-Peppery Dipping Sauce:* **Combine 3 tablespoons** *rice wine vinegar or red wine vinegar,* **2 tablespoons** *soy sauce,* **and 1 tablespoon** *Hot-and-Peppery Oil* **(see recipe, below) or** *chili oil.* **(Note: Chili oil is available in Oriental markets.)**
1 **cup finely chopped bok choy** 1 **cup finely chopped broccoli stems** ⅓ **cup finely chopped bean sprouts** 4 **teaspoons soy sauce** 1 **tablespoon grated gingerroot**	● Stir in the chopped bok choy, the chopped broccoli, the chopped bean sprouts, the soy sauce, and gingerroot. Cover and refrigerate filling until ready to fill potstickers. Makes 4 cups filling for Chinese Potstickers (see recipe, left).	

Pork and Vegetable Filling

1 **pound ground pork** ¼ **cup finely chopped onion**	● In a skillet, cook pork and onion till meat is brown and onion is tender, stirring often to break up pieces of meat. Drain off fat.	*Hot-and-Peppery Oil:* **In a saucepan heat ⅓ cup** *cooking oil* **and 2 tablespoons** *sesame oil* **to 365°. Remove from heat. Stir in 2 teaspoons** *ground red pepper* **till dissolved. Cool; strain into a small bottle. Makes ½ cup. (If desired, for a subtler flavor use ½ cup** *cooking oil* **instead of the ⅓ cup cooking oil and 2 tablespoons sesame oil.)**
1 **cup shredded zucchini** 1 **4-ounce can chopped mushrooms, drained** ¼ **cup shredded carrot** 1 **tablespoon soy sauce** 1 **tablespoon dry white wine** *or* **water** 2 **teaspoons grated gingerroot**	● Stir in the shredded zucchini, the chopped mushrooms, the shredded carrot, the soy sauce, the dry white wine or water, and the grated gingerroot. Cover and refrigerate filling until ready to fill potstickers. Makes 4 cups filling for Chinese Potstickers (see recipe, left).	

Fortune Cookies

¼ cup all-purpose flour
2 tablespoons sugar
1 tablespoon cornstarch
  Dash salt
2 tablespoons cooking oil
1 egg white
1 tablespoon water

● In a mixing bowl stir together flour, sugar, cornstarch, and salt. Add cooking oil and egg white; stir till smooth. Add the water; mix well.

● Make one cookie at a time by pouring 1 tablespoon of the batter on lightly greased skillet or griddle; spread into a 3½-inch circle. Cook over low heat about 4 minutes or till lightly browned. Turn cookie with wide spatula; cook for 1 minute more.

● Working quickly, place cookie on pot holder. Put paper strip* with fortune in center (fold paper, if necessary); fold cookie in half and then fold again over edge of bowl. Place in muffin pan to cool. Repeat with remaining batter. Makes 8 cookies.

***Preparation tip:** Before you start making the cookies, write fortunes on small strips of paper.

Use a little American ingenuity to come up with clever prophecies to tuck inside these American-invented cookies. Do a takeoff on your family's background and surprise eveyone with Italian, Jewish, or Spanish fortunes. Or paraphrase quotes from someone you admire—a French chef, a sailing captain, an author, or an economist. But, most of all, have fun doing it.

Place cookie on pot holder. Put paper strip with fortune in center; fold paper, if necessary.

Fold cookie in half and fold again over edge of bowl. Place in muffin pan to cool until cookie holds its shape.

Mandarin Pancakes

1½ cups all-purpose flour
¼ teaspoon salt
½ cup boiling water
3 tablespoons cold water
2 to 3 tablespoons all-purpose flour

● Stir together the 1½ cups flour and salt. Pour the boiling water slowly into flour, stirring constantly with a fork or chopsticks. Stir till well blended. Stir in the cold water. When cool enough to handle, knead in the 2 to 3 tablespoons all-purpose flour till smooth and elastic (4 to 6 minutes.) Shape dough into a ball. Place the dough back in bowl; cover with damp towel. Let stand for 15 to 20 minutes.

To keep these delicate pancakes moist while you prepare Moo Shu Pork (see recipe, page 32), place them on a baking sheet or in a baking dish and cover with a dry towel or plastic wrap.

● Turn dough out onto lightly floured surface. Form into a 12-inch-long roll. Cut roll into 1-inch pieces. Flatten each piece with your fingers.

Form dough into a roll. Cut into 1-inch pieces. Flatten each piece with your fingers.

Sesame oil, cooking oil, or shortening

● To make pancakes, roll each piece of dough into a 6-inch circle. Brush the entire surface of one side of each pancake lightly with sesame oil, cooking oil, or shortening.

Roll into a 6-inch circle. Brush surface of one side lightly with oil or shortening. Stack 2 pancakes, greased sides together.

● Stack two pancakes together, greased sides together. (These delicate pancakes are always cooked in pairs because, when rolled out, they are too fragile to cook individually.) In a heavy ungreased skillet or griddle cook the pancake stacks over medium heat 20 to 30 seconds on each side or till bubbles appear on surface of pancake (a few golden spots will appear). Quickly remove from pan; gently separate paired pancakes. Repeat with remaining pancakes. Makes 12.

Gently separate cooked pancakes. Place on baking sheet; cover with towel or plastic wrap.

Moo Shu Pork

1 pound boneless pork	● Partially freeze pork; thinly slice into bite-size strips. Set aside.
8 dried mushrooms **¼ cup lily buds** **½ of an 8-ounce can bamboo shoots** **2 to 4 green onions** **Gingerroot**	● Soak mushrooms and lily buds for 30 minutes in enough warm water to cover; squeeze to drain well. Chop mushrooms, discarding stems. Slice lily buds into ½-inch pieces. Set aside. Drain and thinly slice bamboo shoots. Set aside. Slice green onions. Set aside. Grate 2 teaspoons gingerroot. Set aside.
4 beaten eggs **⅛ teaspoon salt** **⅛ teaspoon Szechwan peppercorns, crushed** **1 tablespoon cooking oil**	● Combine eggs, salt, and peppercorns. Heat a 10-inch skillet over high heat; add the 1 tablespoon oil. Add egg mixture. Rotate skillet to evenly distribute the egg. Cook 5 seconds more. Remove egg; thinly slice into bite-size strips.
2 tablespoons cooking oil **¼ cup hoisin sauce** **Mandarin Pancakes** **(see recipe, page 31)** **Hoisin Sauce**	● Preheat a wok (see stir-fry tips, page 7) or large skillet over high heat; add the 2 tablespoons oil. Stir-fry the gingerroot in hot oil 30 seconds. Add half of the pork. Stir-fry 3 to 4 minutes. Remove pork. Stir-fry remaining pork 3 to 4 minutes. Return all pork to wok. Add bamboo shoots, mushrooms, lily buds, green onions, and the ¼ cup hoisin sauce. Cook; stir till heated through. Stir in egg strips. Serve with Mandarin Pancakes and hoisin sauce (see hint, right). Makes 5 or 6 servings.

The fun is in the eating of Moo Shu Pork. To enjoy this flavorful filling tucked inside a Chinese-style crepe, spread hoisin sauce on the unbrowned side of a Mandarin Pancake. Try using a green onion brush. It's a novel tool that doesn't have to be washed. Spoon about ¼ *cup* of the hot pork mixture in the center of the pancake. Sprinkle with green onion strips, if desired, and roll up whichever way you like (see tip, opposite). Serve immediately. Use your fingers to eat the pancakes, and dip them in additional hoisin sauce, if you like.

To make green onion brushes, trim onion ends. At one or both ends, cut 2-inch slits. Place in ice water to crisp and curl.

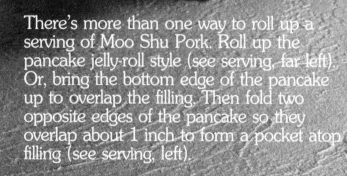

There's more than one way to roll up a serving of Moo Shu Pork. Roll up the pancake jelly-roll style (see serving, far left). Or, bring the bottom edge of the pancake up to overlap the filling. Then fold two opposite edges of the pancake so they overlap about 1 inch to form a pocket atop filling (see serving, left).

Sweet-Sour Chicken

1 large green pepper 1 medium carrot 1 clove garlic	● Cut green pepper into ½-inch pieces; set aside. Thinly slice carrot; set aside. Mince garlic; set aside.
1 8-ounce can pineapple chunks (juice pack) 2 tablespoons cornstarch ⅓ cup honey ⅓ cup red wine vinegar 1 tablespoon soy sauce	● Drain pineapple, reserving juice. Set aside pineapple chunks. Add enough water to the reserved juice to make 1 cup liquid. Stir the 1 cup liquid into the cornstarch. Stir in honey, red wine vinegar, and soy sauce; set aside.
1½ pounds whole chicken breasts, skinned, halved lengthwise, and boned	● Cut the halved and boned chicken breasts into 1-inch pieces; set aside.
1 beaten egg ¼ cup water ¼ cup cornstarch ¼ cup all-purpose flour ½ teaspoon salt	● For batter in a mixing bowl combine egg and water. Add cornstarch, flour, and salt; beat till smooth.
Cooking oil for deep-fat frying	● Dip chicken cubes in batter. Fry the chicken cubes in deep hot oil (365°) for 5 to 6 minutes or till golden. Drain; keep chicken pieces warm.
2 tablespoons cooking oil	● Preheat a wok (see stir-fry tips, page 7) or large skillet over high heat; add the 2 tablespoons cooking oil. Stir-fry garlic in hot oil for 30 seconds. Add green pepper and carrot; stir-fry 3 to 4 minutes.
	● Stir the pineapple juice mixture; stir into wok or skillet. Cook and stir till thickened and bubbly. Cook and stir 1 to 2 minutes more. Add the chicken and the reserved pineapple chunks; heat through. Makes 4 to 6 servings.

Sweet-Sour Chicken is just about one of the prettiest and tastiest stir-frys around. It's also different from most stir-frys because it features deep-fried chicken and plenty of zesty sauce. This all-time favorite is a great introduction to Chinese food for someone who is skeptical of Oriental cuisine. And, if you want to improve your chopstick technique, this dish is easy to eat Chinese-style with its chunky pieces of chicken, green pepper, pineapple, and carrot.

Sweet-Sour Fish

12 ounces fresh *or* frozen
   fish fillets
1 11-ounce can mandarin
   orange sections
1 medium green pepper
4 green onions
   Gingerroot
⅓ cup honey
1 tablespoon cornstarch
⅓ cup vinegar
⅓ cup water
1 tablespoon hoisin sauce

● Thaw fish, if frozen. Remove any skin from fish and cut fillets into 1-inch cubes.

Drain orange sections; set aside. Cut the green pepper into ½-inch pieces; set aside. Slice green onion; set aside. Grate enough gingerroot to make 1 teaspoon.

To prepare sauce, in a small saucepan combine honey and the 1 tablespoon cornstarch. Stir in vinegar, the ⅓ cup water, and hoisin sauce. Cook and stir till thickened and bubbly; set aside.

To keep the fried fish cubes warm, place the drained pieces on a baking sheet lined with paper toweling and keep in a 300° oven till it's time to add them to the stir-fry.

P.S. Use this technique for the Sweet-Sour Chicken (see recipe, opposite), too.

1 beaten egg
¼ cup water
¼ cup cornstarch
¼ cup all-purpose flour
¼ teaspoon salt
⅛ teaspoon five spice
   powder *or* Homemade
   Five Spice Powder
   (see recipe, page 15)
   Cooking oil for deep-fat
   frying
2 tablespoons cooking oil

● For batter, combine the egg and the ¼ cup water. Add the ¼ cup cornstarch, the flour, salt, and five spice powder; beat till smooth.

Dip fish cubes in batter. Fry in deep hot oil (365°) for 3 to 4 minutes. Drain; keep fish pieces warm. Preheat a wok (see stir-fry tips, page 7) or large skillet over high heat; add the 2 tablespoons cooking oil. Stir-fry gingerroot in hot oil 30 seconds. Add green pepper and onion; stir-fry 2 to 3 minutes.

Stir sauce; stir into wok or skillet. Cook; stir till bubbly. Cook and stir 1 to 2 minutes more. Add fish and oranges. Cook; stir 1 to 2 minutes. Serves 4 to 6.

Sweet and Spicy Barbecued Ribs

1 tablespoon brown sugar 1 teaspoon ground red pepper ½ teaspoon salt ½ teaspoon onion powder ¼ teaspoon ground turmeric ¼ teaspoon dry mustard	● In a small bowl combine the brown sugar, the ground red pepper, the salt, the onion powder, the ground turmeric, and the dry mustard.
4 pounds pork loin back ribs *or* spareribs	● Thoroughly rub the ribs with the sugar-spice mixture. Cover and let stand 2 to 3 hours in the refrigerator.
½ cup water ¼ cup hoisin sauce 2 tablespoons molasses 1 tablespoon grated gingerroot	● Meanwhile, for sauce, in a saucepan combine water, hoisin sauce, molasses, and gingerroot; heat to boiling.
	● In covered grill place *medium* coals on both sides of drip pan. Place ribs, bone side down, on grill over drip pan; lower grill hood. Grill ribs 30 minutes. Turn, bone side up, and grill, covered, 30 minutes more. Brush with sauce. Turn, bone side down, and grill 10 to 15 minutes more, brushing generously with sauce. Makes 4 to 6 servings.

It doesn't take any ancient Chinese secret to produce tasty barbecued foods. And a little Western know-how could make your barbecuing efforts more successful. Check the tips below for fire building and see the tip box on page 59 for more barbecuing information.

Mound the briquettes into a pyramid in the center of the firebox. Drizzle liquid lighter or jelly fire starter over the whole surface of charcoal. Wait 1 minute, then ignite with a match. Or use an electric starter. Let the coals burn till they die down to a glow (about 30 minutes). When the coals are ready, use a fire rake or long-handled tongs to spread the coals in a single layer.

Spicy Oven-Baked Spareribs

½ cup water ¼ cup soy sauce ¼ cup plum jelly 3 tablespoons red wine vinegar 1½ teaspoons five spice powder *or* Homemade Five Spice Powder (see recipe, page 15)	● To prepare the marinade, in a small saucepan combine the ½ cup water, the soy sauce, the plum jelly, the red wine vinegar, and the five spice powder or Homemade Five Spice Powder. Cook and stir over low heat till jelly is melted. Cool slightly.
2 pounds meaty pork spareribs, sawed in half across bones	● Cut the meat into single-rib portions. Trim off fat. Place ribs in a shallow baking dish. Pour marinade over ribs; cover. Marinate for 1 hour at room temperature or 2 to 3 hours in the refrigerator, turning ribs occasionally.
	● Drain ribs; reserve marinade. Place ribs, meaty side down, in a foil-lined, large shallow roasting pan. Bake, covered, in a 450° oven for 30 minutes.
1 tablespoon water 1 tablespoon cornstarch ¼ cup thinly sliced green onion	● Meanwhile, prepare sauce. If necessary, add enough water to the reserved marinade to make 1 cup liquid. In a saucepan combine the 1 tablespoon water and the cornstarch. Stir in the reserved marinade and green onion. Cook and stir till thickened and bubbly. Cook and stir 2 minutes more.
	● Drain fat from ribs. Turn meaty side up. Reduce heat to 350°; bake, uncovered, 30 minutes more. Drain fat from ribs, if necessary. Spoon the sauce atop ribs; bake, uncovered, 10 to 15 minutes more. Makes 4 to 6 servings.

Take-out Chinese food is not an American invention. For years many Chinese have bought barbecued specialties at their local restaurant or butcher shop because they had no home oven.

The rib recipes on these two pages let you do the cooking at home, and you can choose your favorite appliance—grill or oven.

Chicken Egg Foo Yung

1 whole small chicken breast, skinned, halved lengthwise, and boned, (½ pound) 1 tablespoon cooking oil 1 cup finely chopped bok choy *or* Chinese cabbage ½ cup chopped green onion	● Using cleaver or knife, finely chop chicken. In skillet or wok stir-fry chicken in the 1 tablespoon hot oil till meat is browned. Drain off fat. Add finely chopped bok choy or Chinese cabbage, and chopped green onion; cook and stir 1 to 2 minutes more. Cool.
1 cup water 4 teaspoons hoisin sauce 1 teaspoon instant chicken bouillon granules 1 teaspoon honey	● To prepare sauce, in saucepan combine the water, hoisin sauce, chicken bouillon granules, and honey. Bring to boiling.
2 tablespoons cold water 1 tablespoon cornstarch	● Stir together the 2 tablespoons cold water and cornstarch; stir into hot mixture. Cook and stir till thickened and bubbly. Turn to low heat; keep warm while frying egg foo yung mixture.
6 eggs ¼ teaspoon salt ¼ teaspoon pepper	● To make egg foo yung, beat together eggs, salt, and pepper. Stir in the cooled chicken-vegetable mixture.
Cooking oil for frying	● In skillet heat about 2 tablespoons oil over medium heat till hot. Using about ¼ cup of the mixture for each patty, fry patties in hot oil about 1 minute per side or till golden. (Spread the chicken-vegetable mixture to cover egg as the egg spreads slightly.) Keep warm. Repeat till all the mixture is used, stirring each time; add more oil as needed. Serve with sauce. Makes 5 or 6 servings.

Trade in your old omelet recipe for Chicken Egg Foo Yung. With its fresh vegetables, chicken, and delightfully sweet brown sauce, it's a refreshing addition to brunch or supper menus.

Egg Drop Soup

| 2 | 14½-ounce cans chicken broth
| 1 | tablespoon cornstarch

● In saucepan slowly stir the chicken broth into cornstarch. Cook, stirring constantly, till slightly thickened.

| 1 | well-beaten egg
| 2 | tablespoons sliced green onion

● Slowly pour in the well-beaten egg; stir gently. Remove from heat. Garnish with green onion. Serves 4.

Gently stir the egg to create the delicate texture of this soup. This Chinese technique is featured on page 57 with our Hot and Sour Soup.

Moo Goo Gai Pan

| 1 | whole large chicken breast, skinned, halved lengthwise, and boned

● Partially freeze chicken; thinly slice into bite-size strips.

| ¾ | cup water
| 3 | tablespoons soy sauce
| 2 | tablespoons dry sherry
| 4 | teaspoons cornstarch
| 1 | tablespoon honey
| 1 | teaspoon instant chicken bouillon granules

● In a small mixing bowl stir together the water, soy sauce, dry sherry, cornstarch, honey, and instant chicken bouillon granules; mix well.

| 1 | 8-ounce can water chestnuts, drained
| 1 | cup fresh pea pods *or* ½ of a 6-ounce package frozen pea pods, thawed
| ½ | cup fresh mushrooms
| 4 | to 6 green onions
| | Gingerroot

● Slice the drained water chestnuts; set aside. Halve the pea pods crosswise; set aside. Slice the mushrooms and the green onion; set aside. Grate 2 teaspoons gingerroot; set aside.

| 2 | tablespoons cooking oil

● Preheat wok (see stir-fry tips, page 7) or large skillet over high heat; add oil. Add the chicken to wok or skillet; stir-fry 3 to 4 minutes. Remove chicken. (Add more oil, if necessary.)
    Stir-fry water chestnuts, pea pods, mushrooms, green onions, and gingerroot 3 to 4 minutes.

● Return chicken to wok or skillet. Stir the bouillon mixture and stir into chicken. Cook and stir till thickened and bubbly. Cover and cook 2 minutes more or till heated through. Serves 4 to 6.

Have you ever thought about ordering Moo Goo Gai Pan in a restaurant, but then changed your mind because you didn't really know what it was? A quick Chinese translation: "Moo Goo" means mushrooms; "Gai" means chicken; and "Pan" means sliced. Put them all together and you have Sliced Chicken with Mushrooms. We've added water chestnuts and pea pods to our version to give it color and crunch.

Vegetable Chow Mein

Once you've tasted our version of chow mein, you will never buy the dump-it-out-of-a-can variety again. Fresh and authentic Chinese ingredients make the extra preparation time worthwhile.

¼ cup lily buds	● Soak lily buds for 30 minutes in enough warm water to cover. Drain; cut lily buds into 1-inch lengths, discarding tough stem ends.
1 medium carrot	● Cut carrot into julienne strips. In a saucepan cook carrot, covered, in boiling water for 4 minutes. Drain well; set aside.
¼ head Chinese cabbage 4 ounces fresh bean curd (tofu) ½ of an 8-ounce can bamboo shoots 1 small onion 1 clove garlic ½ cup peanuts	● Chop the Chinese cabbage; set aside. Cut the bean curd into julienne strips; set aside. Drain the bamboo shoots and halve lengthwise; set aside. Cut the onion into thin wedges; set aside. Mince the garlic; set aside. Set aside the peanuts.
¾ cup cold water 2 tablespoons cornstarch 3 tablespoons soy sauce 2 teaspoons sugar	● Stir water into cornstarch; stir in soy sauce and sugar. Set aside.

2 tablespoons cooking oil
Chow mein noodles, warmed
	● Preheat a wok (see stir-fry tips, page 7) or large skillet over high heat; add cooking oil. Stir-fry onion and garlic in hot oil 1 minute. Add Chinese cabbage; stir-fry 2 minutes. Remove vegetables.
	
	    Add more oil, if necessary. Add bamboo shoots, carrot, and lily buds; stir-fry 2 minutes. Stir soy sauce mixture; stir into wok or skillet. Cook and stir till thickened and bubbly. Add cabbage and onion. Carefully stir in bean curd. Cover and cook 1 minute. Add peanuts; heat through, tossing gently to mix.
	
	    Serve at once over warmed chow mein noodles. Makes 4 to 6 servings.

Chicken Chow Mein

2 whole medium chicken breasts	● Skin, halve lengthwise, and bone chicken. Cut chicken into bite-size pieces; set aside. Chop bok choy; set aside. Chop zucchini; set aside. Chop mushrooms; set aside. Thinly slice celery; set aside. Bias-slice green onions into 1-inch lengths; set aside. Mince garlic; set aside. Grate enough gingerroot to make 1 tablespoon; set aside.
¼ medium head bok choy (about ½ pound)	
1 medium zucchini	
1 cup fresh mushrooms	
1 stalk celery	
6 green onions	
1 clove garlic	
Gingerroot	

1 cup chicken broth	● Stir the chicken broth into the cornstarch. Stir in the dry white wine and the soy sauce; set aside.
2 tablespoons cornstarch	
¼ cup dry white wine	
2 tablespoons soy sauce	

2 tablespoons cooking oil Chow mein noodles, warmed	● Preheat wok (see stir-fry tips, page 7) or large skillet over high heat. Add cooking oil. Stir-fry garlic and gingerroot in hot oil for 30 seconds. Add celery. Stir-fry for 1 minute. Add mushrooms; stir-fry for 1 minute. Remove celery and mushrooms.

Add more oil if necessary. Add zucchini to wok or skillet; stir-fry for 2 minutes. Add bok choy; stir-fry 2 minutes more. Remove zucchini and bok choy.

Add more oil if necessary. Add half the chicken to wok or skillet; stir-fry for 2 minutes. Remove chicken; stir-fry remaining chicken 2 minutes. Return all chicken to wok or skillet. Stir chicken broth mixture; stir into wok or skillet. Cook and stir till thickened and bubbly. Add celery-mushroom mixture, zucchini-bok choy mixture, and onions. Cover and cook for 2 to 3 minutes or till heated through.

Serve at once over warmed chow mein noodles. Makes 6 servings.

"Chow mein" by any other name is "fried noodles"—the literal Chinese translation. Somewhere between the East and West, the long and tender stir-fried noodles of China changed into the crunchy short variety served in Chinese-American restaurants and sold in American supermarkets.

The words, chow mein, refer only to the noodles—not the entire dish. So a dish with fried noodles can have any topper and still be a chow mein. Also, from the Chinese point of view the American term "chow mein noodles" is redundant; that would be the same as saying "fried noodles noodles."

Beef Chop Suey

1 **pound beef top round steak**	● Partially freeze beef; thinly slice across the grain into bite-size strips. Set aside.
2 **cups fresh bean sprouts** *or* **one 16-ounce can bean sprouts** ½ **cup bamboo shoots** ⅓ **cup fresh mushrooms** 1 **medium onion** 1 **small green pepper** 1 **stalk celery** 2 **tablespoons pimiento** 1 **clove garlic** **Gingerroot**	● If using canned bean sprouts, drain well and set aside. Chop bamboo shoots; set aside. Thinly slice mushrooms; set aside. Thinly slice onion and separate into rings; set aside. Chop green pepper; set aside. Chop celery; set aside. Chop pimiento; set aside. Mince garlic; set aside. Grate gingerroot to make 1 teaspoon; set aside.
1½ **cups beef broth** 2 **tablespoons cornstarch** 3 **tablespoons soy sauce** 2 **tablespoons tomato paste** 1 **teaspoon sugar**	● In a small bowl stir beef broth into cornstarch. Stir in soy sauce, tomato paste, and sugar; set aside.
2 **beaten eggs** 1 **tablespoon cooking oil**	● In a 10-inch skillet cook beaten eggs in the 1 tablespoon cooking oil, without stirring, till set. Invert skillet over a baking sheet to remove cooked eggs; cut into short, narrow strips. Set aside.

2 **tablespoons cooking oil**
Hot cooked rice *or* **chow mein noodles, warmed**
Soy sauce (optional)
	● Preheat a wok (see stir-fry tips, page 7) or large skillet over high heat; add the 2 tablespoons cooking oil. Stir-fry garlic and gingerroot in hot oil for 30 seconds. Add onion, green pepper, and celery; stir-fry 1 minute. Add bamboo shoots and mushrooms; stir-fry for 2 minutes. Remove vegetables from wok.
	    Add more oil, if necessary. Add half of the beef to wok or skillet; stir-fry for 2 to 3 minutes or till browned. Remove beef. Stir-fry remaining beef 2 to 3 minutes. Return all meat to wok or skillet. Stir beef broth mixture; stir into wok. Cook and stir till thickened and bubbly. Return bamboo shoots, mushrooms, onion, green pepper, and celery to wok. Add bean sprouts, egg strips, and pimiento. Cover and cook for 2 to 3 minutes or till heated through.
	    Serve chop suey over rice or warmed chow mein noodles. Pass soy sauce, if desired. Makes 6 servings.

Gingerroot (below) is a staple in a Chinese kitchen. For short-term storage, wrap the root in paper toweling and refrigerate. For longer storage, immerse peeled slices of gingerroot in dry sherry and refrigerate in a covered container for up to 3 months. Or freeze unpeeled gingerroot and cut off what you need while it's still frozen.

Pork Chop Suey

1 **pound boneless pork**	● Partially freeze pork; thinly slice into bite-size pieces. Set aside.

2 **cups fresh bean sprouts *or* one 16-ounce can bean sprouts** ¼ **medium head cabbage** ½ **cup water chestnuts** 1 **medium carrot** 1 **medium green pepper** 1 **medium tomato** 6 **green onions**	● If using canned bean sprouts, drain well; set aside. Chop cabbage; set aside. Chop water chestnuts; set aside. Thinly slice carrot; set aside. Cut green pepper into 1-inch pieces; set aside. Cut the tomato into wedges; set aside. Cut the onions into 1-inch lengths; set aside.

½ **cup chicken broth** 2 **tablespoons cornstarch** 2 **tablespoons dry sherry** 2 **tablespoons soy sauce**	● In a small bowl stir chicken broth into cornstarch. Add dry sherry and soy sauce; set aside.

2 **tablespoons cooking oil** **Hot cooked rice *or* chow mein noodles, warmed** **Soy sauce (optional)**	● Preheat a wok (see stir-fry tips, page 7) or large skillet over high heat; add the cooking oil. Stir-fry water chestnuts, carrot, green pepper, and onions in hot oil for 2 minutes or till crisp-tender. Remove vegetables. 　Add more oil, if necessary. Add half of the pork to wok or skillet. Stir-fry for 2 to 3 minutes or till browned. Remove pork. Stir-fry remaining pork 2 to 3 minutes. Return all of the meat to wok. 　Stir chicken broth mixture; stir into wok. Cook and stir till thickened and bubbly. Add bean sprouts, cabbage, water chestnuts, carrot, green pepper, and onions. Cover and cook for 4 to 5 minutes, stirring occasionally. Add tomato; cover and cook for 1 minute more or till heated through. 　Serve chop suey over hot cooked rice or warmed chow mein noodles. Pass soy sauce, if desired. Makes 4 to 6 servings.

Chop suey wouldn't be chop suey without bean sprouts. But, if all sprouts look alike to you, here's how to tell the difference. Most sprouts are delicate and spindly (for example, alfalfa sprouts), but bean sprouts are sturdy, plump, and white. If fresh sprouts are unavailable, use canned sprouts—but don't expect the crisp texture of the fresh ones. Store leftover bean sprouts, covered in water, in the refrigerator no longer than a week.

Deep-Fried Bean Threads

1 ounce bean threads
(cellophane noodles)
Cooking oil for deep-fat
frying

● Fry bean threads (shown at right), a few at a time, in deep hot cooking oil (375°) about 5 seconds or till bean threads puff (shown at far right) and rise to the top. Remove; drain on paper toweling. Makes 4 servings.

Wispy-stranded bean threads balloon into crunchy, transparent threads after deep-frying.

Deep-Fried Rice Sticks

2 ounces rice sticks
Cooking oil for deep-fat
frying

● Fry *unsoaked* rice sticks (shown at right), a few at a time, in deep hot cooking oil (375°) about 5 seconds or just till sticks puff (shown at far right) and rise to top. Drain on paper toweling. Keep warm in oven. (Store uncooked rice sticks in a tightly closed container.)

For a spectacular show, have guests gather round to watch rice sticks puff in an instant.

Boiled Rice

● In a saucepan, mix 2 cups *cold water,* 1 cup *long grain rice,* 1 tablespoon *butter or margarine,* and 1 teaspoon *salt.* Cover with a tight-fitting lid. Bring to boiling; reduce heat. Cook for 15 minutes; do not lift cover. Remove from heat. Let stand, covered, for 10 minutes. Makes 6 (½-cup) servings.

Oven Rice

● In a 1½-quart casserole, stir 1 tablespoon *butter or margarine* into 2¼ cups *boiling water* till melted. Stir in 1 cup *long grain rice* and 1 teaspoon *salt.* Cover and bake in a 350° oven about 35 minutes or till rice is tender. Fluff rice with a fork after 15 minutes. Makes 6 (½-cup) servings.

Microwave Rice

● In a 2-quart non-metal casserole, mix 2 cups *cold water,* 1 cup *long grain rice,* and 1 teaspoon *salt.* Cook in a counter-top microwave oven on HIGH power 6 minutes or till boiling. Stir; cover. Micro-cook for 5 minutes more; stir. Micro-cook, covered, for 3 minutes more. Stir; add 1 tablespoon *butter or margarine.* Cover rice and let stand 5 to 10 minutes. Makes 6 (½-cup) servings.

Beef Fried Rice

¼ **pound cooked beef**	● Slice cooked beef into bite-size strips (should measure about 1 cup); set aside.
1 **medium cucumber** 1 **small onion** 1 **clove garlic**	● Seed and chop the cucumber; set aside. Chop the small onion; set aside. Mince the garlic; set aside.
2 **tablespoons soy sauce** 2 **tablespoons dry sherry**	● Mix soy sauce and sherry; set aside.

2 **tablespoons cooking oil**
 3 **cups chilled cooked rice**
	● Preheat a wok (see stir-fry tips, page 7) or large skillet over high heat; add cooking oil. Stir-fry garlic in hot oil for 30 seconds. Add cucumber and onion; stir-fry for 2 minutes or till crisp-tender.
	    Add beef; stir-fry for 1 minute. Remove beef and vegetables. Add more oil, if necessary.
	    Add rice to the wok or skillet, tossing to heat for 1 minute. Add beef, vegetables, and soy sauce mixture.

2 **beaten eggs**	● Drizzle beaten eggs over rice mixture. Cook, stirring constantly, till eggs are set. Makes 4 to 6 servings.

Fried rice is the Chinese answer for what to do with leftovers. If you don't have leftover rice, start with uncooked rice and use one of the cooking methods on page 44. To judge how much you'll need, keep in mind that 1 cup uncooked long grain rice yields about 3 cups cooked rice, and 1 cup quick-cooking rice yields 2 cups cooked rice. Chill the cooked rice thoroughly before using so the grains will be separate when you cook them again with the other ingredients.

Drizzle the beaten eggs over the mixture of rice, vegetable, and meat.

Stir rice mixture constantly so the eggs are heated and coat the rice.

Yangchow Fried Rice

2 cups water **¼ pound fresh *or* frozen shrimp in shells**	● In saucepan bring lightly salted water to boiling. Add fresh or frozen shrimp. Simmer 1 to 3 minutes or till shrimp turn pink. Drain, shell, and devein. Chop shrimp and set aside.
2 ounces fully cooked ham ** *or* cooked pork** **2 ounces cooked chicken** **½ cup frozen peas** **⅓ cup fresh mushrooms** **2 green onions**	● Finely dice ham or pork and chicken (should measure about ½ cup each ham and chicken); set aside. Thaw frozen peas by running hot water over them for 5 minutes. Finely chop mushrooms; set aside. Thinly slice green onions; set aside.
2 beaten eggs **1 tablespoon cooking oil**	● In a 10-inch skillet cook beaten eggs in the 1 tablespoon cooking oil, without stirring, till set. Invert skillet over a cutting board to remove cooked eggs; cut into narrow short strips.
3 tablespoons soy sauce **2 tablespoons cooking oil**	● In the same skillet cook shrimp, ham or pork, chicken, peas, green onions, mushrooms, and soy sauce in the 2 tablespoons cooking oil about 4 minutes or till mushrooms and onion are tender.
4 cups chilled cooked rice **½ cup fresh bean sprouts** **Soy sauce (optional)**	● Stir in cooked rice, the bean sprouts, and egg strips; heat through. Serve with additional soy sauce, if desired. Makes 6 to 8 servings.

Cook egg as if it were an omelet. Invert cooked egg in skillet over cutting board so egg comes out in one piece.

Cut egg circle into ¾-inch-wide strips. Then cut strips into 2-inch pieces.

Fried Noodles with Ham and Cabbage

8 ounces fresh Chinese egg noodles *or* fine egg noodles	● Cook noodles in a large amount of lightly salted boiling water till tender; drain well. Rinse with cold water; set noodles aside.
½ head Chinese cabbage **½ pound fully cooked ham** **6 green onions** **Gingerroot**	● Thinly slice Chinese cabbage crosswise; set aside. Thinly slice ham into bite-size strips; set aside. Bias-slice onions into 1-inch lengths; set aside. Grate enough gingerroot to make 2 teaspoons; set aside.
1 cup chicken broth **1 tablespoon soy sauce** **5 teaspoons cornstarch**	● In a bowl, combine the chicken broth, soy sauce, and cornstarch. Set aside.
6 tablespoons cooking oil	● In a heavy 10-inch oven-going skillet, heat *2 tablespoons* of the cooking oil over medium heat. Add the noodles to the skillet. Cook noodles for 4 to 5 minutes or till bottom of noodles is lightly browned. Remove noodles from pan by loosening and inverting onto a plate. Add *2 tablespoons* of the cooking oil to skillet. Slide noodles back into pan, browned side up. Cook for 4 to 5 minutes or till bottom of noodles is lightly browned. Remove from heat; keep noodles warm in a 350° oven.

● Preheat a wok (see stir-fry tips, page 7) or skillet over high heat. Add the remaining *2 tablespoons* cooking oil. Stir-fry gingerroot in hot oil for 30 seconds. Add green onions; stir-fry for 1 minute. Add ham and cabbage; stir-fry for 2 minutes. Stir chicken broth mixture; stir into wok or skillet. Cook and stir till thickened and bubbly.

To serve, place the noodles on a warm serving platter. Pour ham mixture over noodles. Serves 4 to 6.

For authenticity, use fresh Chinese egg noodles in this noodle cake. They are available at Oriental markets. However, fine egg noodles work equally well. Look for them in the pasta section of your supermarket.

Confused about just what Chinese cabbage is? The terms Chinese cabbage, Napa cabbage, and celery cabbage all apply to the cabbage pictured here.

Pork Lo Mein

8 ounces fresh Chinese egg noodles *or* fine egg noodles	● Cook noodles in a large amount of boiling salted water till tender; drain. Rinse with cold water. Drain noodles well and set aside.
1 pound boneless pork *or* Chinese Pork Roast (see recipe page 62) 6 green onions 1 clove garlic	● If using boneless pork, partially freeze pork. Thinly slice pork into bite-size strips. Set aside. Bias-slice green onions into 1-inch lengths; set aside. Mince the garlic; set aside.
3 tablespoons oyster sauce 1 tablespoon soy sauce ½ teaspoon sugar	● Combine the oyster sauce, soy sauce, and sugar; set aside.
2 tablespoons cooking oil	● Preheat a wok (see stir-fry tips, page 7) or skillet over high heat; add the cooking oil. Stir-fry green onions and garlic in hot oil for 1 minute. Remove green onion. 　　Add more oil, if necessary. Add half of the pork to the wok or skillet; stir-fry 2 to 3 minutes. Remove pork. Stir-fry remaining pork 2 to 3 minutes. Return all pork to wok or skillet. 　　Add the cooked noodles, onions, and oyster sauce mixture. Using two spatulas or mixing spoons, lightly toss the mixture for 3 to 4 minutes or till noodles are heated through. Serves 4 to 6.

Eat plenty of Pork Lo Mein and you'll be assured a long life—so the Chinese think, since this dish has lots of noodles, a Chinese symbol of longevity.

　Here's a little advice for successfully stir-frying noodles. Keep tossing the noodles as they cook so they are coated by the oyster sauce mixture and heated without becoming crunchy or tough.

Remove the peel, then finely chop the garlic. Keep the cleaver perpendicular to the cutting board.

To crush garlic with a cleaver, place a clove on a cutting board. Using the flat side of your cleaver, press down and forward to loosen the peel.

Stir-Fried Rice Sticks with Shrimp

4 ounces rice sticks **Boiling water**	● Pour enough boiling water over rice sticks to cover; let stand 5 minutes. Drain; rinse in cold water. Drain well.	**If you can't find rice sticks at your local Oriental market, ask for rice noodles or rice vermicelli (same product, different names). These extra-thin, yellowish dried strands usually come packaged in cellophane bags. (We've pictured rice sticks on page 45.)**
¼ pound fresh *or* frozen **shrimp in shells** **½ cup chicken broth** **1 teaspoon cornstarch** **1 tablespoon dry sherry** **1 teaspoon soy sauce**	● Thaw shrimp, if frozen. Peel and devein shrimp. Halve shrimp lengthwise and crosswise. Set aside. Blend chicken broth into cornstarch; stir in sherry and soy sauce. Set aside.	
1 cup fresh pea pods *or* ½ **of a 6-ounce package** **frozen pea pods, thawed** **1 green onion** **Gingerroot**	● Bias-slice pea pods into ½-inch pieces; set aside. Thinly slice green onion; set aside. Grate enough gingerroot to make 1 teaspoon; set aside.	
2 tablespoons cooking oil	● Preheat a wok (see stir-fry tips, page 7) or large skillet over high heat; add oil. Stir-fry gingerroot in hot oil for 30 seconds. Add green onion and stir-fry 1 minute. Add more oil, if necessary. Add shrimp to wok or skillet. Stir-fry 3 to 4 minutes. Add pea pods; stir-fry for 1 minute. Stir chicken broth mixture, and stir into wok or skillet. Cook and stir till thickened and bubbly.	
	● Add the rice sticks. Cover and cook 2 minutes. Uncover; cook, stirring constantly, for 2 minutes or till all the liquid is absorbed. Makes 3 or 4 servings.	

The Cutting Edge

The presentation of food is all-important in Oriental cuisines. The way Chinese cooks cut ingredients not only enhances the beauty of the foods, it also affects their cooking times. Use this photographic dictionary as a reference when cutting ingredients.

Top row (left to right): red pepper, cut into julienne strips; onion wedge.

Second row (left to right): green onion, thinly sliced; caulifower floweret; zucchini, bias-sliced; green pepper, coarsely chopped; onion, thinly sliced and separated into rings.

Third row (left to right): tomato wedges; caulifower flowerets, thinly sliced; zucchini, cut into julienne strips; carrot, bias-sliced; onion, chopped.

Fourth row (left to right): green onion, bias-sliced into 1-inch pieces; radish, thinly sliced; zucchini, halved lengthwise and thinly sliced; carrot, cut into julienne strips; celery, sliced.

A sharp knife or cleaver is essential to precision slicing. Before each use, sharpen the blade with a sharpening steel. With the steel in one hand, hold knife in the other hand almost flat (at a 20-degree angle) against the steel. Draw the blade over the steel, using a motion that goes across and down. Turn blade over; repeat.

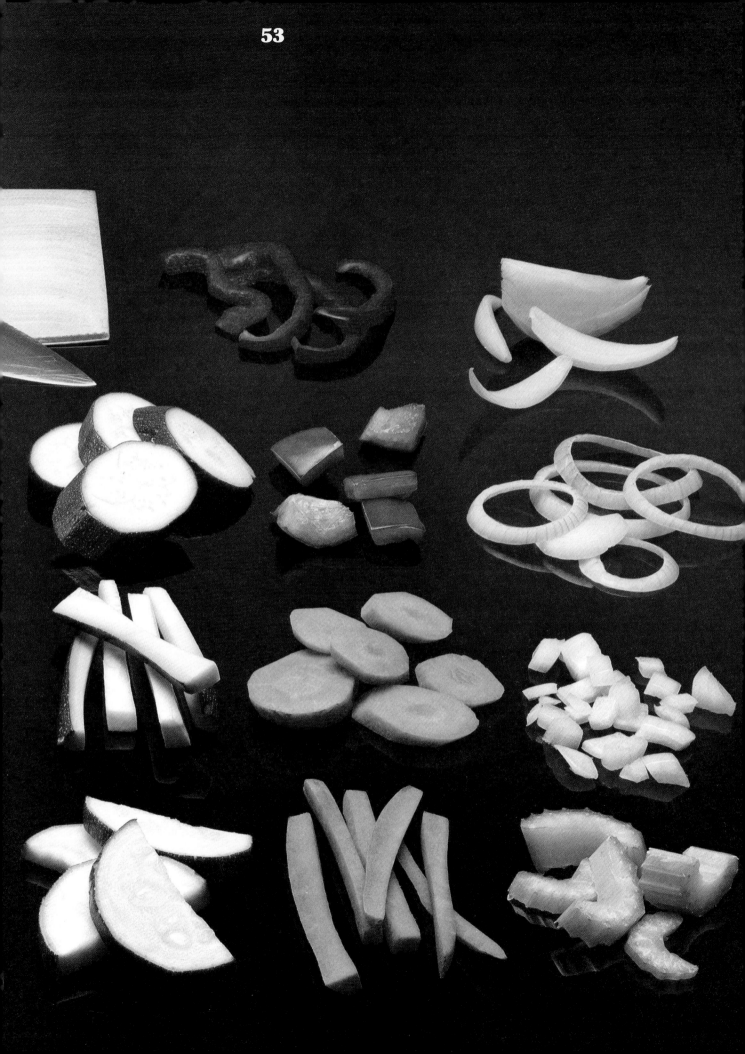

Wonton Soup

8 cups water 20 Wontons (see recipe, page 23)*	● In a large saucepan bring water to boiling. Drop wontons, one at a time, into boiling water. Simmer, uncovered, about 3 minutes. Remove from heat and rinse wontons with cold water; drain thoroughly. Set aside.	**Invite some friends or recruit your family to join in a wonton-wrapping session. Make one or more fillings ahead to have them ready for the helpers when they arrive. Serve the wontons in soup or deep-fry them for a yummy snack (see page 23). Wrap, label, and freeze the extras (if you have any) for soup or snacks another day.**
6 cups chicken broth 1 cup broccoli stems cut into julienne strips 1 15-ounce can straw mushrooms, drained and halved lengthwise 1 teaspoon grated gingerroot	● In the same large saucepan bring the chicken broth to boiling. Add the broccoli strips, the halved straw mushrooms, and the grated gingerroot. Simmer, uncovered, for 5 minutes.	
3 green onions, bias-sliced into 1-inch lengths	● Add wontons and green onions to the saucepan. Heat through. Ladle soup into bowls. Makes 6 to 8 servings.	
	*Note: Choose a filling from the recipes on pages 22-27.	

Rice Patties

Cook ¾ cup *short grain rice** according to package directions (or follow directions on page 44 for cooking rice, *except* omit butter or margarine). Cool. Using about ¼ cup for each, form rice into 8 patties about ½ inch thick. Place on a well-greased baking sheet. Bake in a 300° oven for 1½ hours or till rice appears dried. Carefully remove patties from the baking sheet. In a heavy skillet heat ¼ cup *cooking oil* over medium heat till a kernel of uncooked rice sizzles in the oil. Add patties, a few at a time. Cook over medium heat, turning once, about 30 to 45 seconds per side or till light golden brown. Drain on paper toweling. Keep patties warm in a 350° oven. Makes 8 patties.

*Note: Cooked short grain rice has sticky kernels that hold together better in patties than do other rices.

4 dried mushrooms	● Soak dried mushrooms in enough warm water to cover for 30 minutes; squeeze to drain well. Chop mushrooms, discarding stems.
1 cup cooked shrimp, halved lengthwise **4 cups chicken broth** **½ cup diced cooked chicken** **¼ cup sliced celery** **¼ cup coarsely shredded carrot**	● Coarsely chop shrimp. In a saucepan combine shrimp, broth, chicken, celery, carrot, and mushrooms. Heat to boiling. Reduce heat; keep warm.
8 Rice Patties (see recipe, opposite) **¼ cup sliced green onion**	● Prepare Rice Patties according to recipe directions. Working quickly, place one rice pattie in each soup bowl and pour chicken broth mixture over *or* place all the patties in large serving bowl and pour chicken broth mixture over. (Speed is important to obtain the desired sizzling.) Top with onion. Serves 8.

For a sure-fire conversation starter, serve this talking soup. Pour hot broth over hot rice patties and listen carefully for the sizzling. The Chinese used leftover rice stuck to the bottom of the cooking pot to make their rice patties. Our method (see tip box, opposite) is simpler, and you don't have to scrape the bottom of the pan!

P.S. Fried and salted rice patties make great snacks, too.

Easy Shark's Fin Soup

6 cups chicken broth 1 15-ounce can shark's fin, drained 1 whole medium chicken breast 2 teaspoons grated gingerroot	● In a large saucepan combine the chicken broth, shark's fin, chicken, and gingerroot. Bring to boiling. Reduce heat and simmer, covered, for 20 minutes. Remove from heat. Remove chicken breast; when cool enough to handle, cut off meat and slice into julienne strips. Return meat to soup.
¼ cup dry sherry	● Add sherry to soup. Simmer, covered, 15 minutes more.
1 tablespoon cold water 2 teaspoons cornstarch	● Stir cold water into cornstarch. Stir into soup. Cook soup till slightly thickened and bubbly. Remove from heat. Makes 6 to 8 servings.

The authentic way to make this soup is to soak dried shark fin cartilage for days; our easy way eliminates the soaking by using canned shark's fin.

Poached Fish with Vinegar and Wine Sauce

1 16-ounce package frozen fish fillets, thawed Salt	● Sprinkle fish lightly with salt. Cut fish fillets diagonally into 2x1-inch pieces.
⅓ cup chicken broth 3 tablespoons dry sherry 2 teaspoons rice wine vinegar *or* vinegar	● In a large heavy skillet combine chicken broth, dry sherry, and rice wine vinegar. Bring to boiling; reduce heat. Carefully add all the fish pieces to hot mixture. Simmer fish, covered, for 8 to 10 minutes or till fish flakes easily when tested with a fork. Using a slotted spoon place fish on a heated serving platter.
2 tablespoons water 2 teaspoons cornstarch Thinly sliced green onion	● Stir water into cornstarch; stir into chicken broth mixture in skillet. Cook and stir till thickened and bubbly. Cook and stir 2 minutes more. Pour sauce over fish. Garnish with sliced green onion. Makes 4 servings.

Rice wine vinegar adds a subtle touch to the sauce poured over this poached fish. Look for it in the Oriental section of your market labeled as rice vinegar or rice wine vinegar. Usually it's straw colored, though it can be amber or dark gold. You'll notice it has a sweet flavor unlike many Western vinegars.

Hot and Sour Soup

4 cups chicken broth
½ cup mushrooms, thinly sliced
½ cup bamboo shoots, halved lengthwise
½ cup chopped water chestnuts
2 tablespoons rice wine vinegar *or* white vinegar
1 tablespoon soy sauce
1 teaspoon sugar
½ teaspoon pepper

● In a large saucepan combine the chicken broth, the thinly sliced mushrooms, the bamboo shoots, the chopped water chestnuts, the rice wine vinegar or white vinegar, soy sauce, sugar, and pepper.

Bring chicken broth mixture to boiling. Simmer, covered, for 10 minutes.

A Chinese meal without soup wouldn't be a meal. Soups are the liquid interlude between chopsticksful of rice and other dishes. Traditionally, all diners scoop out of the communal soup bowl throughout the meal whenever they are thirsty.

½ pound frozen peeled and deveined shrimp, thawed
4 ounces fresh bean curd (tofu), cut into bite-size strips

● Halve shrimp lengthwise. Add the shrimp and fresh bean curd to soup. Simmer mixture, covered, for 2 to 3 minutes or till shrimp is done.

1 tablespoon cold water
1 tablespoon cornstarch
1 beaten egg
2 tablespoons finely chopped fresh coriander *or* parsley

● Stir cold water into cornstarch. Stir into soup. Pour egg slowly into hot soup in a thin stream; stir gently till egg cooks and shreds finely.

Continue cooking soup till it's slightly thickened and bubbly. Remove from heat. Stir in chopped coriander or parsley. Makes 4 to 6 servings.

The key to perfect Hot and Sour Soup is to stir the soup gently and keep it just simmering (not boiling) so that the egg forms fine threads rather than turning the soup cloudy or clumping into large pieces.

You'll find both canned straw mushrooms (above) and canned bamboo shoots (right) in Oriental markets. To store unused mushrooms, refrigerate them no more than a week in water in a covered container.

You can buy canned bamboo shoots already sliced, as above, or in a cone-shaped piece that you cut up yourself. Refrigerate unused bamboo shoots up to two weeks in water in a covered container; change the water daily.

Grilled Salmon

¼ cup chicken broth
2 tablespoons finely
   chopped onion
1 tablespoon cooking oil
1 tablespoon soy sauce
1 tablespoon dry sherry
1 tablespoon chopped
   fermented black beans
1 clove garlic, minced

● For marinade, in a saucepan combine the chicken broth, the finely chopped onion, the cooking oil, the soy sauce, the dry sherry, the chopped fermented black beans, and the minced garlic. Bring the mixture to boiling; reduce heat. Simmer, uncovered, for 10 minutes.

3 fresh *or* frozen salmon
   steaks, cut 1 inch thick

● Thaw fish, if frozen. In covered grill arrange *slow* coals around edge of grill. Center a foil pan on grill, not directly over coals. Place fish in foil pan. Brush with marinade. Close grill hood. Grill for 15 minutes. Turn; brush fish with marinade. Grill for 10 to 15 minutes or till fish flakes easily with a fork, brushing occasionally with the marinade. Spoon remaining marinade over fish. Serves 6.

To make your own pan for grilling, use a double thickness of heavy-duty foil.

Sesame Barbecued Pork Chops

2 tablespoons Homemade
  Sesame Paste *or* sesame
  paste
1 tablespoon water
1 tablespoon honey
1 tablespoon soy sauce
1 teaspoon sesame oil *or*
  cooking oil
  Few drops bottled hot
  pepper sauce
6 pork rib chops, cut ¾ inch
  thick

● In a small bowl stir together the Homemade Sesame Paste or sesame paste, the water, the honey, the soy sauce, the sesame oil or cooking oil, and the bottled hot pepper sauce.

Grill pork chops over *medium* coals about 15 minutes. Turn chops; brush with half of the sesame paste mixture. Grill for 15 to 20 minutes more or till well done. Brush on remaining mixture. Makes 6 servings.

Homemade Sesame Paste: Use the steel blade in food processor or use blender. Add ¼ cup *sesame seed.* Cover and process or blend to consistency of fine powder. Add 1 tablespoon *cooking oil.* Cover; process or blend till smooth. Makes 2 tablespoons.

Some cooks suggest that peanut butter works well as a substitute for sesame paste. But since Homemade Sesame Paste is so easy to make, why not enjoy the distinctive flavor it adds to these succulent pork chops?

Barbecue Tip

Successful barbecuing depends entirely on the temperature of the coals. Check the temperature when the coals have burned down to a glow (about 30 minutes after they are ignited). Hold your hand, palm side down, above the coals at the distance the food will be cooking. Start counting, "one thousand one, one thousand two," and so on. If you need to withdraw your hand after 2 seconds, the coals are HOT; 3 seconds, MEDIUM-HOT; 4 seconds, MEDIUM; and 5 or 6 seconds, SLOW.

Smoke Cooking

In China, tea leaves, rice, sugar, or sawdust are burned in the bottom of the wok to smoke foods. The American way, however, is easier and produces similar results. Use a covered barbecue grill and sprinkle the coals with dampened hickory chips. It's safer and requires minimal cleanup. For a bit of Chinese authenticity, place some loose tea in your drip pan (see recipe, right).

Peppery Barbecued Beef

1 2- to 3-pound beef chuck steak, cut 1 inch thick
2 tablespoons Szechwan peppercorns, crushed

● Slash fat edges of steak, being careful not to cut into meat. Press Szechwan pepper into both sides of steak using the heel of your hand or the flat side of a cleaver. Place into shallow baking dish.

½ cup cooking oil
¼ cup hoisin sauce
2 tablespoons soy sauce
2 cloves garlic, minced

● Combine cooking oil, hoisin sauce, soy sauce, and garlic. Pour over steak. Cover; let stand 1 hour at room temperature or 6 hours in refrigerator, turning several times.
 Drain steak, reserving marinade. Grill steak over *medium* coals to desired doneness (allow about 20 minutes on each side for rare or about 25 minutes on each side for medium-rare). Brush occasionally with reserved marinade. Remove meat to a serving platter. Carve across grain into thin slices. Makes 6 to 8 servings.

Add Chinese flair to your next barbecue with Peppery Barbecued Beef—a take-off on steak au poivre. We think you'll like the combination of French-inspired technique with Chinese flavorings and all-American steak.

Salted Smoked Duck

1 tablespoon Szechwan *or* whole black peppercorns, crushed 1 teaspoon finely chopped dried tangerine peel *or* dried orange peel ½ teaspoon salt ½ teaspoon onion salt 1 star anise *or* ½ teaspoon aniseed, crushed	● In a small bowl stir together the crushed Szechwan or black peppercorns, the finely chopped dried tangerine peel or orange peel, the salt, the onion salt, and the crushed star anise or aniseed.	**If you can't find dried tangerine peel at your local Oriental market, make your own following our instructions on page 64. Some Chinese cooks say dried tangerine peel has no substitute, but we think our own version of dried tangerine or orange peel is just as satisfactory.**
1 4- to 5-pound frozen domestic duckling, thawed	● Sprinkle cavity of duck with some of the salt mixture; rub remaining on skin. Let stand 1 hour. In a steamer (see tip, page 67), bring water for steaming to boiling over high heat. Place duck on steamer rack; set rack over boiling water. Cover; steam for 50 minutes.	
3 cups hickory chips ½ cup loose black tea	● Meanwhile, soak hickory chips in water. Place tea in foil drip pan. In covered grill, place *medium-hot* coals on both sides of drip pan. Sprinkle hickory chips over coals. Place duck, breast up, on grill rack above drip pan. Grill about 1½ hours or till done. Using a sharp cleaver or knife, chop duckling, bones and all, into bite-size sections (see illustration, below). Reassemble the duckling into its original whole shape. Serve hot or cold. Makes 3 or 4 servings.	

Carving Chinese-Style

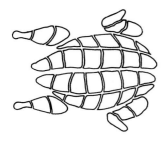

To carve poultry Chinese-style, place the bird breast side up and cut in half lengthwise with a cleaver. Use kitchen shears to finish the cutting. Cut off wings and legs close to the body; set aside. Cut off the backbone on each half of the bird. Cut backbone into bite-size pieces and reassemble on a serving platter. Cut each reserved wing and leg into two or three pieces and arrange on each side of the backbone. Chop the remaining bird halves into bite-size pieces. Reassemble the pieces into the bird's original shape on a serving platter.

Chinese Roast Pork

2 pounds boneless pork shoulder roast	● Cut pork shoulder roast crosswise into 1-inch-thick slices; place in a single layer in a shallow baking dish.

¼ cup hoisin sauce
¼ cup orange juice
2 tablespoons finely chopped onion
1 tablespoon honey
½ teaspoon garlic salt
  Mustard Sauce (see recipe, page 24) *or* bottled plum sauce
Toasted sesame seed

● Stir together the hoisin sauce, orange juice, onion, honey, and garlic salt. Pour over pork. Cover; marinate several hours or overnight in refrigerator, turning once or twice. Drain, reserving marinade.

Place pork slices on rack in broiler pan. Bake in a 350° oven for 50 to 60 minutes or till done; turn and brush occasionally with reserved marinade. Cut meat slices into thin strips.

To serve, dip meat slices into Mustard Sauce *or* plum sauce, then into sesame seed. Makes 8 servings.

Traditionally, Chinese roast pork was a specialty purchased at restaurants or butcher shops. To produce the distinctive flavor, the meat was roasted vertically on hooks in commercial ovens. Our method is much simpler, just as tasty, and you can roast the pork at home.

Making the Most of Your Roast Pork

There's more than one way to use up leftover Chinese Roast Pork. Try the Roast Pork Filling for wontons (see recipe, page 26). The pork-filled wontons are great as appetizers or in Wonton Soup (see recipe, page 54). But our all-time favorite use of leftover Chinese Roast Pork is in Pork-Filled Buns (see recipe, page 69). For moist, juicy buns, save the juices from the roast, but remove all the fat. Then just add the juices to the other filling ingredients.

Salt-Roasted Squab

2 tablespoons soy sauce
2 tablespoons honey
2 tablespoons dry sherry
½ teaspoon five spice
    powder *or* Homemade
    Five Spice Powder
    (see recipe, page 15)
	● In a small bowl stir together the soy sauce, the honey, the dry sherry, and the five spice powder or Homemade Five Spice Powder.	**In China salt roasting is traditionally used with chicken or duck in a pan over an open fire. Try our adaptation with squabs or Cornish game hens in your oven.**

4 12- to 14-ounce squabs *or*
    two 1- to 1½-pound
    Cornish game hens
	● If using Cornish game hens, cut in half lengthwise. Brush birds inside and out with honey mixture. Reserve remaining honey mixture. Wrap each squab or hen half in a single layer of cheesecloth.	

2 pounds coarse salt	● In large heavy oven-going skillet, heat the salt until it is hot. Remove half the salt from the skillet. Place the squabs atop salt in the skillet. Cover with remaining salt. Cover. For squabs, bake in a 350° oven for 45 minutes or till done. (For Cornish hens, bake in a 350° oven for 60 to 65 minutes or till done.) Heat remaining honey mixture and keep warm. Unwrap squabs and brush with honey mixture. Using a sharp cleaver or knife, chop birds into bite-size sections, bones and all (see tip, page 61). Arrange on platter. Makes 4 servings.	**Wrap each squab or hen half in a single layer of cheesecloth and place atop half the heated salt in the skillet.**

Homemade Dried Tangerine Peel

Using a vegetable peeler, thinly slice peel from the rinds of 3 *tangerines or oranges* into 1½x½-inch strips; scrape off excess white. Place strips in a single layer on a baking sheet. Bake in a 300° oven for 7 to 10 minutes for tangerine peel, 10 to 12 minutes for orange peel, or till strips are dried. Store in a covered container. Makes about ⅓ cup peel.

Red-Cooked Chicken

8 dried mushrooms 3 tablespoons dried tangerine peel *or* Homemade Dried Tangerine Peel (see recipe, above)	● In a small bowl soak mushrooms in enough warm water to cover for 30 minutes; squeeze to drain well. Chop mushrooms, discarding stems. Wrap dried tangerine peel loosely in cheesecloth; tie securely.
2 cups water ½ cup soy sauce 1 medium onion, chopped 1 teaspoon grated gingerroot 1 clove garlic, minced	● In a large kettle or Dutch oven, combine the water, the soy sauce, the chopped onion, the gingerroot, the garlic, the chopped mushrooms, and the dried tangerine peel.

1 3½- to 4-pound broiler-fryer chicken	● Place the chicken in the soy sauce mixture. Cover; bring to boiling. Reduce heat; simmer for 25 minutes. Using tongs, turn chicken over. Cover; simmer for 25 to 30 minutes more or till chicken is tender, basting often with the cooking liquid during the last 10 minutes.
	  Remove chicken from pan, reserving cooking liquid. Set chicken aside to cool. When chicken is cool enough to handle, remove meat, discarding bones and skin. Chill chicken and cooking liquid well. Thinly slice chicken; arrange on a platter.
	  Remove tangerine peel from cooking liquid; skim fat. Heat till warm. Pass with chicken. Makes 6 servings.

Somehow, stir-frying and steaming seem to get all the attention as authentic Chinese cooking methods. But here's another technique to add to your culinary skills. Red-cooking is the stewing of meat, poultry, fish, or vegetables in a soy sauce stock that often contains sherry and sugar. It's called red cooking because the soy sauce gives the food a red color. Red-sauced dishes are considered banquet fare, though the recipes featured here are more like American stews. The Chinese are fond of the gravy or sauce the foods are cooked in. It is poured over rice or sopped up with Chinese Flower Rolls (see recipe, page 71).

Snapper with Crabmeat Stuffing

1 2- to 2½-pound fresh *or* frozen dressed red snapper, pike, *or* perch (with head and tail)

● Thaw fish, if frozen. Score fish with about six diagonal cuts on each side, slicing almost through to the bone. (Remove the head or tail, or both if necessary, to fit fish into poacher.)

1 6-ounce can crab meat, drained, flaked, cartilage removed, and finely chopped
½ cup shredded carrot
2 tablespoons thinly sliced green onion
1 teaspoon sugar
1 teaspoon cornstarch
1 teaspoon soy sauce
1 teaspoon dry sherry

● For stuffing, combine the crab meat, the shredded carrot, the thinly sliced green onion, the sugar, the cornstarch, the soy sauce, and the dry sherry.

Fill fish cavity with the stuffing, patting stuffing to flatten evenly. Place fish onto greased rack of a fish poacher. Lower into fish poacher or large kettle.

2 cups water
¼ cup dry sherry
¼ cup soy sauce
1 tablespoon brown sugar
1 teaspoon grated gingerroot

● Combine water, sherry, soy sauce, brown sugar, and gingerroot. Pour over fish. Simmer, covered, 20 minutes or till fish flakes easily. Transfer fish to platter; spoon some cooking liquid atop. Garnish with green onion curls and gingerroot strips, if desired. Serves 4 or 5.

Stuffed snapper is company fare—suitable for a Chinese feast or an American dinner party. Be careful when scoring the fish so it doesn't fall apart as you work with it. The scoring is a Chinese form of food presentation that also allows the red cooking sauce to seep in and flavor the fish.

Beef-Curry Dumplings

2	cups all-purpose flour
2/3	cup boiling water
1/4	cup cold water

● For dough, in a bowl combine flour and boiling water, stirring constantly with a fork or a chopstick. Add cold water; mix with hands till dough forms a ball (dough will be sticky). Cover; set aside.

1	tablespoon soy sauce
1	teaspoon cornstarch
1 to 1½	teaspoons curry powder
1	cup finely chopped bok choy
3/4	cup finely chopped bamboo shoots
2	tablespoons finely chopped onion
1/2	teaspoon salt
3/4	pound lean ground beef

● For the filling, stir the soy sauce into the cornstarch; stir in curry powder.

In a mixing bowl stir together the soy sauce mixture, the finely chopped bok choy, the finely chopped bamboo shoots, the finely chopped onion, and the salt.

Add ground beef; mix well.

● Divide dough in half. Return one half to the covered bowl. Divide the other half into 15 balls; shape according to directions opposite. Shape remaining dough and filling into dumplings.

In steamer bring water for steaming to boiling over high heat. Place dumplings, open side up, on greased steamer rack so dumplings don't touch. (If all dumplings won't fit on steamer rack, refrigerate till ready to steam.) Place steamer rack over boiling water. Cover steamer; steam dumplings 15 to 17 minutes. Makes 30.

Here are a couple of tips to help make your steaming efforts a success. Occasionally check the steamer to make sure it hasn't boiled dry. Add more boiling water as necessary to keep the temperature high. And remember, when removing the lid from a steamer, be careful to let the steam escape away from you. If you don't, the steam buildup can burn you.

Beef Curry Dumplings

To shape the dumplings: Roll each ball on a well-floured surface into a 3-inch circle. Using about 1 tablespoon filling, shape filling into balls and place one in the center of each circle. Bring the dough up around the filling, pleating to fit (see above). Press the dough firmly around the filling. Gently flatten the bottom of each dumpling so the dumplings stand upright by themselves.

Pork-Filled Buns *(see recipe, page 69)*

Making Your Own Steamer

If you don't have a steamer, improvise one by using a wok or Dutch oven. You'll find that your wok's rack for draining fried foods also is ideal for steaming. Or, substitute a round wire cooling rack, a small metal colander, or a foil pie plate with holes punched in it. Pour boiling water into the wok to ½ inch below the rack. To use a Dutch oven, invert a heat-proof bowl into the pan *(see the illustration, right)*. Add water to almost cover the bowl and bring to boiling. Set a round wire cooling rack on top of the bowl.

Steamed Chicken Dumplings

2 cups all-purpose flour **⅔** cup boiling water **¼** cup cold water	● For dough, combine flour and boiling water, stirring constantly with fork or chopsticks. Add cold water; mix with hands until dough forms a ball (dough will be sticky). Cover; set aside.	**There's more than one way to shape a Chinese dumpling. We've used the same technique here as we did for the Chinese Potstickers on page 28. Look there for the illustrations that bring these written directions to life. And, while you're at it, check out the sauces that are served with the potstickers. They're just right with these chicken dumplings.**

1 whole large chicken breast, skinned, halved lengthwise, and boned **½** of a 10-ounce package frozen chopped spinach, thawed and well drained **½** cup finely chopped almonds **¼** cup finely chopped onion	● Finely chop the skinned and boned chicken breast. In a large mixing bowl stir together the finely chopped chicken, the thawed and drained spinach, the finely chopped almonds, and the finely chopped onion.

1 tablespoon oyster sauce **1** tablespoon soy sauce **1½** teaspoons cornstarch **1** teaspoon grated gingerroot	● In a small bowl stir the oyster sauce and the soy sauce into the cornstarch. Stir in the grated gingerroot. Stir into the chicken mixture; set aside.

● Divide dough in half. Return half of dough to covered bowl. On well-floured surface roll other half to about a 1/16-inch thickness. Cut with 2½-inch round cutter. Place a scant 1 teaspoonful of chicken mixture in center of each dough circle. Lightly moisten edges of dough; bring dough up around filling and pinch together to seal.

Flatten bottoms so sealed edge stands upright. Repeat with remaining dough and filling.

In steamer bring water for steaming to boiling over high heat. Place dumplings on greased steamer racks so sides don't touch. Set steamer rack over boiling water. Cover; steam 15 minutes. Makes about 48.

Pork-Filled Buns

3¼ to 3¾ cups all-purpose
   flour
1 package active dry yeast
1¼ cups milk
1 tablespoon sugar
1 tablespoon cooking oil
½ teaspoon salt

● In mixer bowl combine *1½ cups* of the flour and the yeast. In a small saucepan heat milk, sugar, 1 tablespoon cooking oil, and salt just till warm (115° to 120°). Add to flour mixture. Beat at low speed of electric mixer for ½ minute, scraping sides of bowl constantly. Beat 3 minutes at high speed. Using a spoon, stir in as much of the remaining flour as you can. Turn out onto lightly floured surface. Knead in enough of the remaining flour to make a moderately soft dough that is smooth and elastic (3 to 5 minutes). Shape into a ball. Place in a lightly greased bowl, turning once to grease surface. Cover and let rise in warm place till double (45 to 60 minutes). Punch down; turn out on lightly floured surface. Shape into 10 balls. Cover; let rest 5 to 10 minutes.

Not sure what Pork-Filled Buns should look like? We have two photos to help you out. On page 67 you'll find the buns sharing steamer space with the Beef Dumplings. And look for them in the Dim Sum lunch shown on pages 86 and 87.

¼ cup finely chopped
   mushrooms
2 tablespoons thinly sliced
   green onion
1 clove garlic, minced
1 tablespoon cooking oil
½ cup finely chopped
   Chinese Roast Pork
   (see recipe, page 62)
   or cooked pork

● In a small skillet cook the finely chopped mushrooms, the thinly sliced green onion, and the minced garlic in 1 tablespoon cooking oil till onion is tender but not brown.
   Stir in the finely chopped Chinese Roast Pork or cooked pork.

1 tablespoon soy sauce
1 tablespoon dry sherry
2 teaspoons cornstarch

● In a small saucepan stir soy sauce and sherry into cornstarch; cook and stir till thickened; add to pork mixture.
   On a lightly floured surface, roll each ball of dough into a 3½-inch circle. Place a rounded teaspoon of pork mixture in center of each dough circle. Bring edges of dough up around filling, stretching a little till edges *just* meet; pinch to seal. Cover; let buns rest for 10 minutes.
   Meanwhile, in steamer, bring water for steaming to boiling over high heat. Place buns, seam side down, on lightly greased steamer racks so sides don't touch. (If all buns won't fit on steamer rack, refrigerate some while others steam.) Place steamer rack over boiling water. Cover steamer; steam buns 15 to 17 minutes. Makes 10.

Parsley-Coated Beef Balls

1 **slightly beaten egg**
1 **tablespoon sesame seed, toasted**
1 **tablespoon cornstarch**
1 **tablespoon soy sauce**
½ **teaspoon Roasted Szechwan Salt-Pepper (see recipe, page 20)***
1 **pound lean ground beef**
10 **water chestnuts, sliced into thirds**

⅔ **cup finely chopped Chinese parsley *or* parsley**

● In a mixing bowl stir together the egg, the toasted sesame seed, the cornstarch, the soy sauce, and the Roasted Szechwan Salt-Pepper.

Add ground beef; mix well. Shape about 1 tablespoon of the meat mixture around each water chestnut slice.

● Roll meatballs in parsley. Meanwhile, in a steamer bring water for steaming to boiling over high heat. Position meatballs on greased steamer rack so sides don't touch. Place rack over boiling water. Cover; steam for 20 minutes. Serves 6.
*Note: If desired, use 1 tablespoon soy sauce for the salt-pepper.

Chinese parsley (below, left) goes by two other aliases—coriander and cilantro. Shop for it at Italian, Oriental, or Latin-American food stores. Though it resembles parsley (below, right), Chinese parsley has a stronger flavor and fragrance.

Chinese Flower Rolls

1⅓ to 1⅔ cups all-purpose
   flour
  1 package active dry yeast

● In a mixer bowl combine ½ *cup* of the flour and the yeast.

Though flower rolls are traditionally served at banquets, they're an attractive addition to any meal—Chinese or American. Customarily, the rolls are made by rolling two layers of dough jelly-roll style. We short-cut that method, yet achieve the same delicate flower-petal effect.

½ cup milk
  2 tablespoons cooking oil
  1 tablespoon sugar
 ¼ teaspoon salt
  2 tablespoons finely
    chopped green onion

● Heat the milk, oil, sugar, and salt just till warm (115°-120°); stir constantly. Add to flour mixture. Beat at low speed of electric mixer ½ minute, scraping bowl constantly. Beat 3 minutes at high speed. Stir in green onion. Using a spoon, stir in as much remaining flour as you can.

On a lightly floured surface knead in enough remaining flour to make a moderately stiff dough that is smooth and elastic (6 to 8 minutes total). Shape into a ball. Place into a lightly greased bowl; turn once. Cover; let dough rise in warm place till nearly double (about 1 hour). Punch dough down; divide in half. Cover; let rest for 10 minutes.

1 tablespoon sesame oil *or*
   cooking oil

● Roll half of the dough into an 8x6-inch rectangle. Brush sesame oil over rectangle. Roll up jelly-roll style, beginning from one of the shorter sides; seal seams. Cut into four 1½-inch-wide pieces. Using a chopstick, make an indentation in the center of the top of each piece parallel to the cut edges (see below). Press firmly till edges slightly fan out. Repeat with remaining dough. Cover; let rise in warm place till nearly double (25 minutes). In a steamer bring water for steaming to boiling over high heat. Place rolls on greased steamer rack so sides don't touch. Set rack over boiling water; cover. Steam rolls for 20 minutes. Serve warm. Makes 8.

Eight Precious Pudding

8	ounces pitted whole dates, snipped (1⅓ cups)
¾	cup water
½	teaspoon vanilla

● In a small saucepan, combine dates and the ¾ cup water; bring to boiling. Cook, stirring constantly, till water is absorbed. Stir in the ½ teaspoon vanilla; set aside to cool.

3	cups water
1½	cups short grain rice
1	teaspoon salt
1	teaspoon vanilla
¼	cup sugar
2	tablespoons butter *or* margarine, cut up

● In another saucepan, combine the 3 cups water, rice, salt, and the 1 teaspoon vanilla. Bring to boiling; reduce heat. Cook, covered, for 15 minutes or till water is absorbed. Stir in the sugar and butter or margarine.

¼	to ½ cup diced mixed candied fruits and peels
10	to 12 blanched whole almonds

● Meanwhile, decoratively arrange mixed candied fruits and peels in bottom of a buttered 1½-quart casserole or heat-proof bowl. (Make sure casserole or bowl is at least 1 inch smaller than steamer rack.) Arrange almonds in ring around candied fruits and peels. Carefully spoon *half* of the rice mixture into casserole or bowl, being careful not to disturb fruit and nut design. Pat rice up around sides of casserole or bowl to form shell. Mix remaining rice with date mixture. Spoon into rice shell; pat surface even. Cover casserole tightly with foil.

Almond Glaze (see recipe, right)

● In a steamer (see tip, page 67), bring water for steaming to boiling over high heat. Place casserole or bowl on steamer rack over boiling water. Cover and steam 45 to 60 minutes. Carefully unmold hot pudding. Serve pudding warm with Almond Glaze. Makes 10 to 12 servings.

Almond Glaze: In a small saucepan, combine ¼ cup *sugar* and 1 tablespoon *cornstarch.* Stir in 1 cup *cold water.* Cook and stir till thickened and bubbly. Cook and stir 2 minutes more. Remove from heat; stir in 1 tablespoon *butter or margarine* and a few drops *almond extract.*

Traditionally, Eight Precious Pudding is Chinese banquet fare made with exotic Oriental fruits and a sweet bean paste filling. Our version uses candied fruits and a date filling.

Eight Precious Pudding (see recipe, above)

Sugared Nuts (see recipe, page 74)

Chinese New Year Cakes
(see recipe, page 74)

Sweet-Filled Wontons
(see recipe, page 75)

Chinese New Year Cakes

Pictured on pages 72 and 73.

1½ cups all-purpose flour ¼ cup sugar 2 teaspoons baking powder ½ teaspoon salt	● Combine flour, sugar, baking powder, and salt.
2 beaten eggs ⅓ cup water *or* milk 1 tablespoon cooking oil	● Stir together eggs, water or milk, and the 1 tablespoon cooking oil. Add to flour mixture all at once and stir just till moistened.
⅔ cup sesame seed	● Drop batter by tablespoonfuls into a bowl of sesame seed; turn to coat. Place sesame-coated cakes on waxed paper. Let stand 15 minutes.
Cooking oil for deep-fat frying	● Fry, several at a time, in deep hot oil (365°) for 2½ to 3 minutes or till puffy and golden. Drain on paper toweling. Serve warm. Makes 20.

You need not wait for Chinese New Year to serve these tender fried cakes. They make a delicately sweet ending to any meal—Chinese or American.

Sugared Nuts

Pictured on pages 72 and 73.

¾ cup sugar ¼ cup water 1 teaspoon finely snipped Homemade Dried Tangerine Peel (see recipe, page 64) *or* dried tangerine peel ¼ teaspoon ground cinnamon Dash salt 2 cups walnut *or* pecan halves	● In a skillet or wok combine sugar, water, tangerine peel, cinnamon, and salt. Bring mixture to a full rolling boil. Boil gently for 4 minutes, stirring frequently. Remove from heat. Quickly stir in nuts, just till nuts are well coated. Turn mixture out onto waxed paper or foil. Using 2 forks, quickly separate the nuts into bite-size clusters. Cool thoroughly before serving. Makes about ¾ pound.

If you want to be really authentic, use walnuts rather than pecans for this Oriental candy. Eat the sugared nuts as a snack between meals as the Chinese do.

Sweet Filled Wontons

Pictured on pages 72 and 73.

¾ cup canned sweet red
  bean paste
½ cup chopped raisins
⅓ cup coconut
1 tablespoon lemon juice
1 tablespoon water
1 teaspoon vanilla
40 wonton skins *or* 10 egg
  roll skins, cut in
  quarters

● For filling, in a mixing bowl stir together the sweet bean paste, the chopped raisins, the coconut, the lemon juice, the water, and the vanilla. For each wonton, position wonton skin with one point toward you. Place about 1 teaspoon of filling just off center of skin. Fold bottom point of wonton skin over filling; tuck point under filling. Roll once to cover filling, leaving 1 inch unrolled at the top of skin. Moisten the right-hand corner of skin with water. Grasp the right and left corners of skin; bring these corners toward you below the filling. Overlap the left-hand corner over the right-hand corner; press the wonton skin securely to seal (see photograph, page 23). Repeat to make 40 wontons.

Here's an authentic Chinese sweet for you-- wontons filled with sweet bean paste. Take a trip to your local Oriental market to stock up on this unusual ingredient made from pureed red beans and sugar.

Cooking oil for deep-fat
  frying
Powdered sugar

● Fry wontons, a few at a time, in deep hot oil (365°) for 2 to 3 minutes or till golden. Drain on paper toweling. Cool. Dust with powdered sugar. Makes 40.

Tea Serving Tips

Teatime is just about anytime in China—with the exception of a meal. Then soup serves as the necessary liquid. Traditionally, tea is drunk often during the day, and when guests come. Though it is not customarily drunk with a meal, tea may be served as the ending to a meal since desserts are virtually unknown in China. Since most Americans would rather not fuss with single cups of tea at meal time, here are directions for tea by the potful made from leaves: Warm a teapot by rinsing it with boiling water. Measure 3 to 6 teaspoons *loose black, green, or oolong tea leaves* into a tea ball. (These teas are the three basic types available in China.) Empty teapot; add tea ball to pot. Immediately add 4 cups *boiling water* to teapot. Cover pot and let steep 3 to 5 minutes. Remove tea ball; stir tea and serve at once. Makes 6 (6-ounce) servings.

Candied Fruit Slices

¾ cup all-purpose flour
½ cup ice water
1 beaten egg

● In a mixing bowl prepare batter by combining flour, ice water, and egg; beat till smooth.

2 medium apples *or* firm bananas
Cooking oil for deep-fat frying

● Peel and core apples; cut into ⅜-inch-thick slices (or peel bananas and cut into 1-inch-thick chunks). Drop apples or bananas, a few pieces at a time, into prepared batter; turn to coat well. Fry apple slices or banana pieces, a few at a time, in the deep hot oil (365°) for 1 to 2 minutes or till lightly golden. Drain on paper toweling.

1 cup sugar
1 cup light corn syrup
½ cup water
2 tablespoons cooking oil

● At serving time, prepare syrup by combining sugar, corn syrup, water, and the 2 tablespoons cooking oil in a 1½-quart saucepan. Bring to boiling over medium heat; stir till sugar dissolves. Continue boiling, stirring occasionally, till mixture turns light caramel color (280° on candy thermometer). Immediately turn heat to *low*.

Ice water

● Working very quickly, dip fruit pieces in hot syrup to coat, then *drop* into a large bowl of ice water. Remove at once to a buttered serving platter (some syrup will go unused; see tip at right for clean-up). Serve *immediately* because the candy glaze will soften if allowed to stand. Makes 4 to 6 servings.

While you're enjoying these sweet treats, the leftover syrup in the saucepan will harden. But cleanup is easy. Just fill the syrup-coated saucepan with water and heat till the syrup melts enough to clean the pan.

For a truly spectacular confectionary delight, serve Candied Fruit Slices. Treat this dessert as the specialty it is and show it off to guests. Fry the batter-coated fruit pieces ahead. Then after dinner, gather guests around you in the kitchen to observe the coating process (and to help, too, if they'd like!). While you're heating the syrup, have one guest ready the ice water and another butter the serving platter. That way the fruit will be ready for dunking and serving immediately after you coat it with the syrup.

Spicy Oven-Baked Spareribs (see recipe, page 37)

Chinese Salad (see recipe, page 80)

Chinese Dinner for Eight

To make dinner a leisurely occasion and preparation manageable, this menu features traditional Chinese foods served in four American-style courses—appetizer, soup, salad and entrée, and dessert.

Ginger Beef with Oyster Sauce (see recipe, page 80) and Oven-Baked Rice (see recipe, page 44)

MENU
Spicy Oven-Baked Spareribs
Egg Drop Soup
Chinese Salad
Ginger Beef with Oyster Sauce
Oven-Baked Rice
Pear-Almond Buns   Tea
Wine: Cabernet Sauvignon

MENU COUNTDOWN
3 Hours Ahead:
Marinate Spicy Oven-Baked Spareribs; chill. Prepare vegetables and dressing for Chinese Salad; chill. Chop vegetables for Ginger Beef with Oyster Sauce; chill. Prepare Egg Drop Soup except for egg; chill. Prepare Pear-Almond Buns.

1½ Hours Ahead:
Bake spareribs and make sauce.
45 Minutes Ahead:
Marinate meat for entrée.
During Dinner:
Before serving spareribs, put soup on the range at low heat and put rice in the oven. To serve soup, stir in egg at the last minute. Before dessert, reheat buns in the oven and make a pot of tea.

Pear-Almond Buns
(see recipe, page 81)

Egg Drop Soup
(see recipe, page 39)

Chinese Salad

Pictured on pages 78 and 79.

2 small zucchini 2 medium carrots 1 medium Chinese white radish Peppery Dressing (see recipe, opposite)	● Cut zucchini, carrots, and radish into julienne strips. In small amount of boiling salted water cook carrots for 2 minutes. Add zucchini; cook 2 minutes more or till vegetables are just tender. Drain and add to radish. Cover and chill. Pour Peppery Dressing over vegetables; toss to coat. Makes 8 servings.

The Japanese call it daikon; the Chinese call it a white radish. If your grocery store or Oriental market doesn't have a white radish, you can substitute a white turnip or icicle radish.

Ginger Beef with Oyster Sauce

Pictured on pages 78 and 79.

1½ pounds beef top round steak	● Partially freeze beef; thinly slice across the grain into bite-size strips.
3 tablespoons oyster sauce 2 tablespoons dry white wine 4 teaspoons cornstarch 1 teaspoon sugar ¾ cup cold water	● For marinade, combine oyster sauce, white wine, cornstarch, and sugar. Mix well. Add beef; stir to coat. Let stand 30 minutes at room temperature. Drain meat; reserving marinade. Set aside. Add water to reserved marinade.
1 medium red *or* green pepper 1½ cups fresh bean sprouts 1 medium onion Gingerroot	● Slice pepper into julienne strips; set aside. Set aside bean sprouts. Chop onion; set aside. Grate gingerroot to make 1 tablespoon; set aside.

2 tablespoons cooking oil	● Preheat wok (see stir-fry tips, page 7) or large skillet over high heat. Add cooking oil. Stir-fry gingerroot in hot oil for 30 seconds. Add onion and stir-fry for 1 minute. Add pepper; stir-fry 1 minute. Remove pepper and onion. Add bean sprouts, stir-fry 1 minute. Remove bean sprouts.
	    Add more oil if necessary. Add *one-third* of the beef to hot wok or skillet; stir-fry 2 to 3 minutes or till browned. Remove beef. Stir-fry another *third* of the beef 2 to 3 minutes. Remove beef. Stir-fry remaining beef for 2 to 3 minutes. Return all meat to wok or skillet.
	    Stir reserved marinade and stir into beef. Cook and stir till thickened and bubbly. Stir in cooked vegetables. Cover and cook 2 minutes or till heated through. Makes 6 to 8 servings.

Show off your stir-frying style by preparing Ginger Beef with Oyster Sauce at the table in an electric wok. (You might want to practice your technique first, using some of the other stir-fry recipes in this cook book.) The key is to make sure all the ingredients are ready to go before you start. Just place the marinated and drained beef, the pepper strips, the bean sprouts, and the chopped onion in separate bowls and tuck them in the refrigerator until your guests arrive.

Peppery Dressing

2 tablespoons rice wine
  vinegar *or* vinegar
2 tablespoons hoisin sauce
1 teaspoon sesame oil
½ teaspoon Hot and Peppery
  Oil (see recipe, page 29)
  or chili oil

● In small bowl stir together the rice wine vinegar or vinegar, hoisin sauce, sesame oil, and Hot and Peppery Oil or chili oil. Cover and chill till serving time. Makes ¼ cup.

Peppery Dressing can add pizzazz to any combination of chilled vegetables. This recipe will generously coat about 4 cups vegetables.

Pear-Almond Buns

Pictured on page 78.

1½ to 1¾ cups all-purpose
  flour
1 package active dry yeast
½ cup milk
2 tablespoons cooking oil
1 tablespoon sugar
¼ teaspoon salt

● In a mixer bowl combine ½ *cup* of the flour and the yeast.
  Heat milk, oil, sugar, and salt just till warm (115° to 120°). Add to flour mixture. Beat at low speed of electric mixer ½ minute, scraping bowl. Beat 3 minutes at high speed. Using a spoon stir in as much remaining flour as you can. Turn out onto a lightly floured surface. Knead in enough remaining flour to make a moderately soft dough (3 to 5 minutes total). Place in a lightly greased bowl; turn once. Cover; let rise in warm place till double (about 1 hour).

The Chinese wouldn't eat sweet buns for dessert—they'd rather have them for a between-meal snack. But we think your guests will like these unusually light rolls as an ending to your dinner. If you don't have a steamer to cook the buns, see our tip for a steamer substitute on page 67. To make this an easy-on-the cook dessert, just make the buns a few hours ahead. Then at dessert time wrap them in foil and warm them in a 325° oven about 10 minutes or till buns are heated through.

⅓ cup finely chopped dried
  pears
2 tablespoons warm water
¼ cup toasted, finely
  chopped almonds
2 tablespoons brown sugar

● Meanwhile, for filling, combine pears and water; let stand 20 minutes. Stir in almonds and brown sugar.
  Punch dough down; turn out onto a lightly floured surface. Shape into 12 balls. Cover; let rest 10 minutes. On a lighty floured surface roll each ball of dough into a 3-inch circle. Spoon about 1 tablespoon of the filling mixture on each dough circle. Bring edges of dough up around filling, stretching till edges just meet; pinch to seal. Cover buns, let rest 10 minutes.
  Meanwhile, in steamer over high heat bring water for steaming to boiling. Place buns, seam side down, on lightly greased steamer rack so sides don't touch. Place rack over boiling water. (If all buns won't fit on steamer rack, chill remaining until ready to steam.) Cover steamer; steam rolls for 20 minutes. Makes 12.

Hot Pot Dinner for Six

Gather friends around the hot pot for a change-of-pace dinner. Rent or borrow this exotic utensil that uses hot charcoal to keep a flavorful broth bubbly for cooking bite-size pieces of meat or fish. Later, serve guests the broth as soup. End the meal with this Chinese-inspired fruit tart and plum wine (see recipes, pages 84 and 85).

MENU
Chrysanthemum Hot Pot
Chinese Fruit Tart
Wine: Plum wine

MENU COUNTDOWN
6 hours ahead:
Prepare Chinese Fruit Tart; chill.
1 hour ahead:
Prepare meat/fish platter, cube bean curd, and slice Chinese cabbage for Chrysanthemum Hot Pot; chill. Make Soy-Vinegar Dipping Sauce.
30 minutes ahead:
Build fire in hot pot. Soak bean threads.

Chrysanthemum Hot Pot

Pictured on pages 82 and 83.

½ **pound beef top round *or* sirloin steak**
½ **pound boneless pork**
1 **whole medium chicken breast, skinned, halved lengthwise, and boned**
½ **pound fresh *or* frozen scallops**

● Partially freeze beef and pork. Thinly slice across the grain into bite-size slices. Cut chicken into bite-size pieces. If using frozen scallops, thaw.

Arrange beef, pork, chicken, and scallops on platter. Cover platter and refrigerate till serving time.

***Soy-Vinegar Dipping Sauce:* In a bowl combine 3 tablespoons *soy sauce,* 3 tablespoons *Chinese black vinegar* or *rice wine vinegar,* and 1 thinly sliced *green onion.* Makes ⅓ cup.**

2 **ounces bean threads (cellophane noodles) Hot water**

● In a large bowl pour hot water over bean threads to cover; let stand 30 minutes. Drain well; squeeze out excess moisture. Cut bean threads into 2-inch lengths; set aside.

● About 30 minutes before serving, line a heatproof pan with heavy-duty foil. Place charcoal briquettes in a pile. Outdoors or in a well-ventilated area, drizzle liquid lighter over the entire surface of briquettes. Wait 1 minute, then ignite with a match. (Charcoal is ready to use when flame dies down to a glow and no areas of black show.)

8 **cups chicken broth**
3 **cups sliced Chinese cabbage**
3 **cups small fresh spinach leaves**
1 **cup fresh bean sprouts**
4 **ounces fresh bean curd (tofu), cut into ½-inch cubes**
  Chrysanthemums (optional)
  Soy-Vinegar Dipping Sauce (see recipe, right)

● In a large saucepan bring the chicken broth to boiling. Stir in cabbage, spinach, bean sprouts, and bean curd. Spoon some of the broth mixture into firepot. Keep extra broth mixture warm and replenish firepot as necessary. Cover the firepot. One at a time, carefully place the hot charcoal briquettes down the chimney of the firepot and rest them on the grate. (Or, use a metal fondue pot instead of a firepot. Pour broth into metal fondue pot till about half full; heat to boiling on range top. Transfer to fondue burner.)

Meanwhile, if desired, place stemmed fresh chrysanthemums on serving platter.

To serve, use chopsticks or forks to dip desired meat or fish into boiling broth mixture. Allow about 2 minutes cooking time for each piece. Then dip into Soy-Vinegar Dipping Sauce. Add additional broth mixture to firepot as necessary. When all meats and fish have been eaten, add bean threads to broth; ladle broth mixture into individual soup bowls. Makes 6 servings.

Chinese Fruit Tart

Pictured on pages 82 and 83.

1 cup all-purpose flour	● In a mixing bowl combine the flour and ¼ teaspoon salt. Cut in butter and shortening with a fork (or pastry cutter) till mixture resembles coarse crumbs. Make a well in the center. Beat together the 1 egg yolk and water. Add to flour mixture. Using fork, stir just till dough forms a ball. Knead 3 or 4 times. Wrap in clear plastic wrap and chill 20 minutes in freezer or 1½ hours in refrigerator. On floured surface roll dough into a 13-inch circle. Fit dough into an 11-inch flan pan, pressing bottom and sides gently to remove any air bubbles. Turn overlapping dough edges to inside and press against sides of pan. Prick sides with fork. (If dough is quite soft, freeze dough in flan pan for 30 minutes.) Line the bottom and sides of pie shell with heavy-duty foil; fill with dry beans. Bake in a 400° oven for 20 minutes. Remove foil and beans. Bake about 5 minutes more or till golden. Cool thoroughly in pan on wire rack. Transfer the baked shell to platter, if desired.
¼ teaspoon salt	
¼ cup cold butter *or* margarine	
1 tablespoon shortening	
1 egg yolk	
2 tablespoons cold water	

A little French, a little American, a little Chinese—that's the best way to describe this refreshing dessert. The buttery-rich flan crust is definitely an import from Western Europe. And the filling uses one of the West's most favorite ingredients—cream cheese. For the fruit topping, the exotic loquats and lychees represent the East. (The loquats are orange-colored; the lychees are off-white.) For a truly authentic Chinese dessert (with a little lighter touch), serve lychees or loquats over crushed ice.

⅓ cup sugar	● In saucepan combine sugar, the 2 tablespoons cornstarch, and ¼ teaspoon salt. Gradually stir in the milk. Cook and stir till thickened and bubbly; remove from heat. In small bowl combine cream cheese and the 3 egg yolks. Gradually stir cream cheese mixture into the hot mixture, stirring constantly. Return mixture to heat; cook and stir 2 minutes more. Remove from heat. Stir in vanilla. Cover surface with clear plastic wrap; cool without stirring. Spread cooled mixture into baked shell; chill.
2 tablespoons cornstarch	
¼ teaspoon salt	
1¼ cups milk	
1 3-ounce package cream cheese, softened	
3 beaten egg yolks	
1 teaspoon vanilla	

1 8-ounce can pineapple tidbits (juice pack)	● Drain pineapple tidbits, reserving juice. Add water, if necessary, to make ½ cup liquid. Halve lychees and loquats. Decoratively arrange the pineapple tidbits, halved lychees, and halved loquats atop pudding layer.
1 11-ounce can whole pitted lychees, drained	
1 11-ounce can whole pitted loquats, drained	

1 teaspoon cornstarch	● For glaze, in saucepan combine the reserved pineapple juice and the 1 teaspoon cornstarch. Cook over medium heat, stirring constantly, till thickened and bubbly. Cook 2 minutes more. Spoon or brush glaze over fruit. Chill 1 to 2 hours. Makes 8 servings.

Dim Sum for Eight

This co-op lunch lets you try many Chinese foods without a lot of work. Have each guest bring a dish to finish preparing in your kitchen. Allow plenty of time for lunch because guests will prepare foods between courses.

MENU

First Course
    Paper-Wrapped Bundles
    Chinese Beer or Tea
Second Course
    Spicy Barbecued Chicken
        Wings
    Chinese Potstickers with
        Beef and Vegetable Filling
Third Course
    Wonton Soup using Wontons
        with Vegetable Filling

Fourth Course
    Pork-Filled Buns
    Chilled Noodle Salad
Fifth Course
    Chinese New Year Cakes
    Pineapple spears

MAKE-AHEAD TIPS AND
PARTY COUNTDOWN
(see pages 88 and 89)

Chilled Noodle
Salad (see recipe,
page 88)

Chinese New Year Cakes
(see recipe, page 74)

Pork-Filled Buns
(see recipe, page 69)

Wonton Soup using Wontons with Vegetable Filling (see recipes, pages 22, 23, and 54).

Paper-Wrapped Bundles (see recipe, page 88)

Above: Chinese Potstickers with Beef and Vegetable Filling (see recipes, pages 28 and 29) and Spicy Barbecued Chicken Wings (see recipe, page 88)

Spicy Barbecued Chicken Wings

12 chicken wings	● Cut off and discard wing tips; separate wings at joints to make 24 pieces.
¼ **cup soy sauce** ¼ **cup dry sherry** 2 **tablespoons cooking oil** 1 **tablespoon honey** ½ **teaspoon onion powder** ½ **teaspoon five spice powder *or* Homemade Five Spice Powder (see recipe, page 15)**	● For marinade, combine soy sauce, sherry, cooking oil, honey, onion powder, and five spice powder or Homemade Five Spice Powder. Place chicken in shallow dish; pour marinade over. Cover and marinate in refrigerator several hours or overnight. Drain, reserving marinade.
	● *To broil:* Place the chicken wings on unheated rack of broiler pan. Broil the chicken wings 3 inches from heat for 8 minutes. Brush with some of the marinade. Turn chicken. Broil about 8 to 10 minutes more, brushing occasionally with reserved marinade. *To grill:* Place chicken wings over *medium-hot* coals. Grill chicken for 15 minutes. Turn chicken. Grill 10 to 15 minutes more. Brush chicken often with reserved marinade during the last 10 minutes of grilling. Makes 24.

Chilled Noodle Salad

4 ounces fresh Chinese egg noodles	● Cook noodles according to package directions; drain well. Cover with *ice water;* let stand till noodles are chilled. Drain well.
6 medium radishes, cut into thin strips ⅓ **cup sliced green onion**	● In a bowl combine noodles, radishes, and onion; set aside.
3 **tablespoons soy sauce** 2 **tablespoons rice wine vinegar *or* vinegar** 1 **tablespoon cooking oil** 2 **teaspoons honey** ½ **teaspoon Hot and Peppery Oil (see recipe, page 29) *or* chili oil**	● For dressing, in a screw-top jar combine the soy sauce, the rice wine vinegar or vinegar, the cooking oil, the honey, and the Hot and Peppery Oil or chili oil. Cover and shake to mix well. Pour over noodle mixture; toss to mix. Cover; marinate in refrigerator 6 hours or overnight. Drain off dressing. Makes 4 to 6 servings.

MAKE-AHEAD TIPS

Use these tips to help organize your dim sum lunch and to help your guests assemble their assigned foods.
Host **(1st Course):**
Prepare Paper-Wrapped Bundles up to one hour before the party; chill. (Or, prepare only the ingredients for bundles; let guests wrap their own.)
Guest 1 **(1st Course):**
Chill beer ahead.
Guest 2 **(2nd Course):**
Prepare ½ recipe *uncooked* Chinese Potstickers with Beef and Vegetable Filling; freeze till final preparation.
Guest 3 **(2nd Course):**
Several hours or the night before, marinate the chicken wings; chill.
Guest 4 **(3rd Course):**
Prepare Wontons using Vegetable Filling for Wonton Soup up to one day ahead and place on baking sheet or tray; chill. Cut up vegetables for soup up to one day ahead; chill.
Guest 5 **(4th Course):**
Prepare Pork-Filled Buns up to one day ahead. Wrap in foil; chill.
Guest 6 **(4th Course):**
Prepare Chilled Noodle Salad up to one day ahead; chill.
Guest 7 **(5th Course):**
Prepare Chinese New Year Cakes up to one day ahead. Wrap in foil. Just before party, prepare pineapple; chill.

Paper-Wrapped Bundles

1 tablespoon hoisin sauce
1 tablespoon soy sauce
1 teaspoon grated
    gingerroot
½ teaspoon honey
¼ teaspoon salt
2 cloves garlic, minced
½ pound fresh *or* frozen
    shrimp, shelled,
    deveined, and cut in
    half lengthwise
½ cup fresh bean curd (tofu),
    cut into ½-inch cubes
1 medium carrot, cut into
    2-inch julienne strips

● For the marinade, in a small deep bowl combine the hoisin sauce, soy sauce, gingerroot, honey, salt, and garlic; mix well.

Add shrimp and bean curd to marinade. Marinate at room temperature 30 minutes, stirring occasionally. Drain.

Cook carrots in small amount of boiling salted water for 1 to 2 minutes or till crisp-tender; drain.

½ of a 10-ounce package
    frozen cut asparagus,
    thawed
½ cup sliced fresh
    mushrooms
    Parchment paper, cut into
    8-inch squares

● Divide shrimp, bean curd, carrot, asparagus, and mushrooms evenly among parchment squares, placing ingredients in center of squares. For each square, bring two opposite sides of square together at top. Fold down edges in series of locked folds. Roll up each end in a series of locked folds. (Tightly crease edges to secure folds.)

Cooking oil for deep-fat
    frying

● Fry the parchment bundles, a few at a time, in deep hot oil (365°) for 1 to 1½ minutes. Drain on paper toweling.

To eat, unwrap the parchment paper using a fork or chopsticks. Makes 8.

● **Variations for the filling:** In place of shrimp, use 1 whole large *chicken breast,* skinned, halved lengthwise, boned, and cut into bite-size strips; *or* ½ pound boneless *pork,* partially frozen and cut into bite-size strips.

PARTY COUNTDOWN

Your lunch party will run smoothly if you follow these guidelines. Prepare the foods for each course just before they are eaten so all the guests can eat together.

Before First Course:
Host: Fry bundles you or guests have wrapped. *Guest 1:* Prepare tea or serve chilled beer.

Before Second Course:
Guest 2: Cook frozen potstickers. *Guest 3:* Grill or broil chicken wings.

Before Third Course:
Guest 4: Assemble ingredients for soup; heat through. *Guest 5:* Preheat oven to 350° for buns.

Before Fourth Course:
Guest 5: Reheat buns in the oven for 8 to 10 minutes. *Guest 6:* Drain salad; place in serving container or on platter.

Before Fifth Course:
Guest 7: While guests are eating fourth course, reheat cakes in a 350° oven for 20 to 30 minutes. Place pineapple spears in serving bowl. **Note:** Keep all foods chilled until their final preparation time.

Chicken with Chinese Sausage Stuffing (see recipe, page 93)

Green Tea Ice Cream (see recipe, page 92)

Winter Melon Soup with Crabmeat (see recipe, page 92)

Chinese-American Dinner for Four

Even though this dinner looks and eats All-American, authentic Chinese ingredients add a subtle Oriental touch to the soup, chicken, and ice cream. Complete the meal with your favorite fruit salad, rolls, and vegetable.

MENU
Winter Melon Soup with
  Crabmeat
Chicken with Chinese Sausage
  Stuffing
Fruit salad
Steamed asparagus *or* carrots
Dinner rolls
Green Tea Ice Cream
Wine: Rosé

MENU COUNTDOWN
5 hours ahead:
Prepare Green Tea Ice Cream; ripen 4 hours in ice cream freezer.
3 hours ahead:
Prepare and bake Chicken with Chinese Sausage Stuffing. Prepare fruit salad; chill.

1 hour ahead:
Prepare Winter Melon Soup with Crabmeat; heat when guests arrive. If desired, wrap asparagus spears or carrot strips with 6-inch lengths of green onion top. Cook asparagus and heat rolls during the soup course.

Winter Melon Soup with Crab
Pictured on page 91.

| 2 | cups chicken broth |
| ¼ | cup dry white wine |

● In a large saucepan combine the chicken broth and wine.

1½	cups diced, peeled winter melon
1	6-ounce can crab meat, drained, flaked, and cartilage removed
¼	cup thinly sliced bamboo shoots

● Add the peeled and diced winter melon, the drained and flaked crab meat, and the thinly sliced bamboo shoots. Cover and simmer for 15 to 20 minutes or till winter melon is tender. Season with salt and pepper. Serves 4.

There's no substitute for winter melon, and you'll know why after tasting this delicate soup. Ask for the melon at Oriental markets. It's also known as bitter melon.

Green Tea Ice Cream
Pictured on page 90.

| 1 | tablespoon loose green tea |
| 1½ | cups cold water |

● Place tea leaves in a tea ball. Quickly bring cold water to a full rolling boil. Meanwhile, warm a teapot by rinsing with some additional boiling water. Place tea ball in teapot; pour the 1½ cups boiling water into teapot. Cover; steep 5 to 10 minutes. Remove tea ball. Chill.

1½	cups sugar
¼	cup all-purpose flour
½	teaspoon salt
2½	cups milk
4	beaten eggs

● In a 3-quart saucepan combine sugar, flour, and salt. Stir in milk. Cook and stir over medium-high heat till slightly thickened and bubbly. Gradually stir about 1 cup hot mixture into eggs. Return to hot mixture. Cook and stir 1 minute. Chill.

Here's a dessert whose flavors are so subtle that your guests may have a hard time guessing what they're tasting. But tea drinkers and non-tea drinkers alike are bound to enjoy the creamy richness of this Chinese-inspired dessert.

4	cups whipping cream
¼	teaspoon finely shredded lemon peel
⅛	teaspoon ground nutmeg
10	to 12 drops green food coloring (optional)

● Stir in chilled green tea, whipping cream, lemon peel, nutmeg, and green food coloring, if desired.

● Freeze in a 4- or 5-quart ice cream freezer according to manufacturer's directions. Makes about 3½ quarts.

Chicken with Chinese Sausage Stuffing

Pictured on page 90.

4 dried mushrooms	● Soak dried mushrooms in enough warm water to cover for 30 minutes; squeeze to drain well. Chop mushrooms, discarding stems. Set aside.
¼ cup thinly sliced green onion **1 tablespoon sesame oil *or* cooking oil**	● Meanwhile, in saucepan cook the onion in the sesame oil or cooking oil till tender but not brown.
⅔ cup chicken broth **⅓ cup long grain rice** **1 tablespoon soy sauce** **1 tablespoon dry sherry** **¼ teaspoon ground ginger**	● Add chicken broth, rice, soy sauce, sherry, and ginger. Bring to boiling. Reduce heat. Cook 15 minutes; do not lift cover. Remove from heat; let stand, covered, for 10 minutes.
½ cup sliced Chinese sausage *or* cubed smoked sausage (about 3 ounces) **½ cup chopped pitted red dates *or* pitted whole dates** **⅓ cup sliced water chestnuts**	● Stir in the sliced Chinese sausage or smoked sausage, the chopped pitted dates, the sliced water chestnuts, and the chopped mushrooms.
1 2½- to 3-pound whole broiler-fryer chicken	● Spoon some of the stuffing into neck cavity of chicken. Skewer neck skin to back. Spoon remaining stuffing into body cavity. Tie legs securely to the tail and twist the wing tips under back of chicken. Place bird, breast side up, on rack in a shallow roasting pan.
¼ cup soy sauce **1 tablespoon cooking oil**	● Combine soy sauce and cooking oil; brush over chicken. Roast, uncovered, in a 375° oven about 1½ hours or till drumstick moves easily in socket. Makes 4 to 6 servings.

If you know someone who says he hates Chinese food, try out this recipe on him. We've taken all-American chicken and packed it full of a subtly flavored rice stuffing that uses some of the more unusual Oriental ingredients around. The result is a terrific dish sure to please Eastern or Western palates.

Index